S0-DTA-333

DAYDREAMS

DAYDREAMS

MAKING YOUR FANTASIES WORK FOR YOU

BY DAVID COLLINS

Franklin Watts
New York | London | 1979

"He Loves and She Loves" by Ira Gershwin & George Gershwin.
Copyright © 1972 NEW WORLD MUSIC CORPORATION
Copyright Renewed
All Rights Reserved
Used by Permission of WARNER BROS. MUSIC

"You Are Too Beautiful" by Lorenz Hart & Richard Rodgers.
Copyright ©1932 RODART MUSIC CORPORATION
Copyright Renewed
All Rights Reserved
Used by Permission of WARNER BROS. MUSIC

"Dancing In The Dark" by Howard Dietz & Arthur Schwartz.
Copyright ©1930 WARNER BROS. INC.
Copyright Renewed
All Rights Reserved
Used by Permission

"Everything's Coming Up Roses" by Stephen Sondheim.
Copyright © 1959 by Norbeth Productions, Inc. and Stephen Sondheim;
Stratford Music Corporation & Williamson Music, Inc., owners of
    publication & allied rights for the Western Hemisphere.
Chappell & Co., Inc., sole selling agent
International Copyright Secured
All Rights Reserved
Used by permission

"All Of You" by Cole Porter.
Copyright © 1954 by Cole Porter
Copyright Renewed, assigned to John F. Wharton as Trustee of the
    Cole Porter Musical & Literary Property Trusts;
Chappell & Co., Inc., owner of publication & allied rights.
International Copyright Secured
All Rights Reserved
Used by permission

Library of Congress Cataloging in Publication Data

Collins, David, 1932-
    Daydreams : making your fantasies work for you.

    Includes index.
    1. Success. 2. Fantasy—Therapeutic use.
I. Title.
BF637.S8C54   154.3   78-31733
ISBN 0-531-09907-5

Copyright © 1979 David Collins
All rights reserved
Printed in the United States of America
5 4 3 2 1

CONTENTS

To my family and friends—
leading characters
in my happiest fantasies

DAYDREAMS

INTRODUCTION

We can never really know one another. However chatty, voluble, communicative we may be, we show and tell pretty much what we choose. An excess of love or fright or drink might cause us to part with a bit more than usual. But inevitably our total dimensions lie concealed.

There's simply too much going on in our heads to share everything. Thoughts bounce off walls. Images flash about. Responses click. And moment to moment what surfaces from the deep must serve to establish our identity. But much more is going on. Most interesting are those ongoing little entertainments that dance in and out of the shadows. In our waking moments they crowd our consciousness, engage our attention, submit to our control, and invite us to become impresarios of our own theater of the mind. We call them daydreams, or fantasies. They are a very private part of us. And a very important part.

We are the stars of our fantasies, or, at the very least, we share top billing with our friends and foes. Our desires and curiosities, fears and anxieties inspire the plots, and in them we find ourselves doing things we wouldn't *dream* of doing in real life. Or doing things we *would* do if life would be a bit more generous. We don't often talk about them with others, perhaps because they seem too silly, embarrassing, or bewildering.

They can also make us feel guilty. Grown-ups aren't supposed to spend their time daydreaming. There's work to be done.

"'Barbara, stop daydreaming and get dressed.' I can hear my mother saying it now," a friend, Barbara Vann, told me. "I daydreamed a great deal as a child," she continued, "and I have a very clear memory of myself getting dressed in the morning, sitting on the edge of my bed, putting on my socks, and drifting off into some fantasy or other.

"It was a pattern. In the morning. While I was putting on my socks. Obviously it was a pattern my mother knew, because her 'Barbara, stop daydreaming,' was as much a part of my morning as 'breakfast is ready.'"

Barbara's mother was, in a way, passing along a cultural taboo. As psychologist Eric Klinger observed in his recent book *Structure and Function of Fantasy* (Wiley, 1971), "Western civilization has long placed the highest value on active, willed reason. . . . Indeed the West is oriented toward action outward, not toward contemplation of inner experience."

The tendency of our culture to devalue inner experience, and defer the study of inner events, together with Freud's tendency to identify daydreams with neurosis, have discredited fantasy as a healthy activity for adults. For years we have considered it improper, a waste of time, at best a bearly tolerable indulgence for adolescents. ("Barbara, stop daydreaming!")

But in the last decade daydreams and fantasies have gained a new and positive image. Reevaluation began in 1966 when psychologist Jerome Singer published his book *Daydreaming* (Random House). It was the first American work to devote itself exclusively to the psychological examination of fantasy, and the first Western work of its kind since Varendonck's *The Psychology of Daydreams*, published in 1921. Its positive reinterpretation of the significance of fantasy in our lives sparked strong new interest in its study.

Subsequent study and research programs have substantiated that daydreaming is a normal function of the healthy adult mind, and that many of us spend a large number of our waking moments in fantasy. It appears our daydreams can tell us much about our inner selves. They can relieve psychic pressures, and aid us in problem solving and decision making. They can even be used as tools to reshape our lives.

The daydreams described in this book illustrate some of the principal ways fantasies can work for us. Not the least of these ways is that they entertain us. Many of the daydreams recorded here are pure entertainment, as amusing for us as for their creators. Their subjects range widely. As they grew in number, it became apparent that they fell into certain general categories.

Fantasies of being beautiful, of being near or possessing someone or something beautiful are the focus of chapter I. Fantasies of falling in love, being in love, getting married, staying married, or losing love are the subject of chapter II.

Sex fantasies curl the pages of chapter III. Lust for power and money—and our fears of losing them—spark the fantasies discussed in chapter IV. Some of the most fiendish and funny daydreams are in chapter V, all about revenge. Pursuits of glory, fame, and heroism win the day in chapter VI.

Getting out of it all, dying, breaking free and going to hell are the focus of the fantasies in chapter VII. And chapter VIII charts the course of another life: our perfect, idealized existence, in heaven, Shangri-la, a new world.

I spoke with many people in the course of gathering the material for this book—friends, associates, acquaintances, strangers. Some said they didn't daydream, and I believed them. Some said they didn't daydream, and I didn't believe them. Almost everyone said they did daydream and, with a little coaxing, they related at least one choice fantasy, which is presented here under a pseudonym.

These fantasies were often related in touching ways.

Sometimes, as I asked and probed, I had the feeling my "subjects" were reaching into some secret garden from which, after some introspection, they would carefully choose a prized flower and hand it to me, sometimes shyly, sometimes with great aplomb.

My approach to this book is journalistic, rather than scientific. Although I did attempt to select fantasies from all age groups, no effort was made to get an even sampling from varied social, economic, and educational backgrounds.

No strict technique was used in the recording of the fantasies. Where my tape recorder could be used easily and well, it was used. More often, conversations were taken down in note form and extensively edited and restructured into monologues that preserved as accurately as possible the subject's language and narrative ability.

The subjects were all highly capable and functioning adults, and were all, with a few possible exceptions, reasonably contented individuals, with what I guessed to be an average share of pluses and minuses in their lives. In most cases, I encouraged each person to relate points of interest from his or her background that had direct bearing on their fantasy activity. As our conversations touched on possible interpretations and meanings of their fantasies, I encouraged them to venture their own opinions and feelings.

Where it seemed appropriate and to the point I have quoted briefly from a few prominent theorists and researchers in the field, and from those whose work has bearing on our understanding and enjoyment of the subject.

In some cases, where those whom I quote have published their work in both books and magazines, I have tended to quote from their magazine articles, from which, for the purposes of this book, their points were more easily excerpted.

As is the custom in this field of study, I have used the terms *daydream* and *fantasy* interchangeably, with perhaps some preference for the term *daydream* for the more mundane images, and *fantasy* for the more bizarre.

If *Daydreams* has a point or purpose, it is to share and spread in an enthusiastic and, I hope, responsible way the good news that we are creatures who not only indulge in, but also benefit from daydreaming, and that we do so in every phase of our lives, from childhood to our later years.

It is important that we be realistic about ourselves and the world around us, and that we live and move forward in that real world. But so much of what happens to us, and what we make happen *for* us, happens in our heads first. We visualize, we fantasize what our life can be, and if we are skillful and determined and capable of commitment, we can bring that life into being. Fantasies can be like lanterns that light our progress, show us the way, offer us role models for our behavior, provide us with valuable mental rehearsals for real achievement.

If we choose a positive image of ourselves, and vividly imagine the achievement of positive goals we set for ourselves, then set to work to achieve those goals, we can make our lives a heartening series of dreams coming true.

Along the way our daydreams can lighten our labors with their power to amuse and delight, to ease our anxieties and fears, to indulge our curiosities and desires, to help us sift through and evaluate what our scanners pick up each waking moment.

If we get to know and enjoy and use our fantasies more, we will get to know and enjoy and use ourselves better. In the following pages fantasies are related that show how a few of us approach the art.

I. BEAUTY

If on the other hand, I'm faithful to you,
It's not through a sense of duty.
You are too beautiful
And I am a fool for beauty.

Lorenz Hart
"You Are Too Beautiful"

Beauty has been making fools of us since time began. Beautiful men and women have been turning heads, breaking hearts, even starting wars since we first began exchanging glances. Few of us, at some point in our lives, have not wanted to be beautiful, have not felt love, or envy, or even hate for those who possess it.

We know its power. We have known it since we were children. It made a difference among us then. And those of us who most keenly felt its lack turned to wit and muscle and guile to compete. Yet whatever our accomplishment, the competition seemed unfair. Beauty just had to stand there. The rest of us had to keep moving.

Florenz Ziegfeld gave the possession of beauty an enthusiastic twentieth-century perspective. In his introduction to a beauty book of the 1920s, *Secrets of Charm*, by Josephine Huddleston, he wrote:

> It is the last true thrill left us in a mechanized age. It is a precious gift that cannot be standardized. Everything else is routined and regulated and ordered, but beauty cannot be had for the asking. The gods bestow it where they will.

And where the gods bestowed it, Ziegfeld discovered it, glorified it, packaged and sold it as the fantasy of the all-American blond. His spectacular revues ushered in an era of the idealization of blond beauty. Other fantasy makers followed his lead. MGM sold it as Jean Harlow. Twentieth-Century-Fox sold it as Marilyn Monroe. Clairol sold it as Born Blonde. And we bought it—lock, stock, and peroxide—this terrific fantasy of blond beauty, of blondes having more fun. Some of us became blond and had more fun, especially if we really believed golden locks could produce a good time.

Most of us daydream. Some of us can build quite elaborate fantasies. Sometimes we borrow the fantasies that artists and merchants construct for us. For centuries they have played on our desires to be beautiful, to possess beauty. They have made us delirious with their images. Paintings, poems, sculptures, songs, photographs, novels, films have teased, catered to, and sated our appetite for beauty. Indeed, beauty is so relentlessly exploited that it is small wonder those of us who do not possess it to any striking degree can be made to feel inadequate, can be driven to fantasies of possessing great beauty.

Barbara's favorite fantasy, which she has worked on over a period of years, is elaborate and grand-scaled. It is typical of many in that it is rooted in a prepackaged fantasy. But she embroidered it artfully on her own. Barbara is a handsome woman in her middle thirties, with a fine smile, great poise, and a sense of humor.

Barbara

"This one started years ago. It's grown a lot over the years. I'm sure it got started with all those MGM musicals about Ziegfeld and his showgirls. When they show them on TV, I still look for them and enjoy them. In my fantasy, I am a showgirl, of course. *The* showgirl, as a matter of fact. The one who comes on last. And is the most spectacular. It usually begins backstage. The big finale has begun.

Someone is singing one of those pretty-girl numbers, and a bevy of beauties has already started down the grand staircase. I come out of my dressing room. A maid, or dresser of some sort, is fussing around me, putting the last touches on my costume. I'm almost nude, but there's a lot going on with diamonds and feathers. And a huge headdress.

"The thing of the show is that the featured showgirls—there are four of us—a brunette, two blondes, and a redhead—are brought to the top of the grand staircase by an elevator that comes up from the basement. Up comes this big, mirrored elevator. The doors part, and out steps Miss Gorgeous at the top of the staircase. And down the stairs she starts. Meanwhile, the elevator descends to pick up the next Miss Gorgeous.

"So, anyway, when I'm downstairs coming out of my dressing room, I talk to the other girls, and, one by one, they disappear into the elevator, saving me, the best, of course, for last. The other featured showgirls are close personal friends, both in the fantasy, and in real life. That is, I've brought in some attractive friends to join in the fun. And I mean *fun*, for I'm aware throughout that I'm exhilarated, very good-humored, really enjoying showing off. By the way, we're all—my friends and me—about six inches taller than we are in real life. Our busts are a little fuller, our hips a bit rounder, our legs a bit straighter, the works.

"I'm very aware throughout that I am the star, the most breathtaking one saved for last. I am enjoying the admiring glances of everyone backstage. Then it's my turn to get into the elevator. My maid is still fussing with me right up to the last minute. I am aware of composing myself. Then the doors close, and I go up. A few seconds later, I am at the top, the doors slide open, and I step out onto the top of the staircase in a very graceful, showgirly way. Ta-*da*!

"I pose for a second. The audience gasps. Applause! I smile radiantly. Then I begin to descend the staircase, very stylishly, very carefully. The music builds to a big crescendo. I arrive at the bottom of the staircase, move to the footlights. The other girls group in around me. The audience is applauding wildly.

"I usually stop the fantasy about there. Sometimes I think about some handsome guy waiting for me in my dressing room. Usually somebody I know. Or want to get to know. But that's about it. Fade out."

Barbara didn't need Florenz Ziegfeld. She made herself a star. She used Ziegfeld's format to present herself gloriously as something ravishing to behold. But she wrote her own scenario to personalize it, even peopled it with friends to make her exalted position more natural and comfortable. For one or two shining moments, glittering in the spotlight, she can embody absolute beauty. Savor its glory. Taste its power. Contemplate her conquests.

"When the fantasy is over," says Barbara, "I feel euphoric. The image carries over for a while in real life. I have the feeling of being looked at, of being quite special. I compose my face, walk and talk self-consciously, some-what with the feeling of, well, here I am, so extraordinary-looking, yet somehow moving about, *living*, just like ordinary people.

"Then it wears off, like Novocain. I may make a few passes in front of a mirror, and make a few mental notes about reviving my exercises, or doing my hair differently, or trying some new eyelashes, but basically it's over, and I'm just plain Barbara again. Well, not *plain* Barbara, but you know what I mean. Just me."

Barbara emphasized again this was a daydream she'd been playing with for years. When asked how often she "ran" it, she said she couldn't be sure, but probably three or four times a year. When I asked her if she remembered anything specific that triggered it, she replied:

"Not really. But I'm sure it must have been at moments I was feeling...frumpy, or was not attracting someone I wanted to attract. Or was just bored."

A lively imagination is a sure cure for boredom. And much more. Leading researchers and theorists in the field of fantasy today hold that our daydreams and fantasies perform many useful tasks in our everyday lives. They can be home entertainment. Problem solvers. Outlets for pent-up frustration. A quick high. Indicators of current concerns. Carriers of recurring fears, doubts, frustrations. Scenarios of dominant personality traits. Exposers of submerged aspects of our egos. And more.

Barbara and I talked about other possible motivations for her fantasy. Fear of aging was one: an important one in a world where the good life would seem to be reserved for those with younger-looking skin. Barbara continues:

"But I don't think I'm really hung up on the age thing. I think we're all getting a bit tired of the youth-cult bull. At least here I am in my middle thirties, and I'd better not be hung up on it. Anyway, I don't think I ever really relied on my good looks as a passport to anything. I'm no great beauty. But I'll admit I've always been glad I wasn't born homely.

"I have a career [she is a real estate agent]. And much of my ego goes into that. But here's something, speaking of career. At times, when things get a little tough, or some kind of problem comes up that I wish I didn't have to cope with, I do think: 'I wish I didn't have to put up with this. There must be an easier way.' What easier way than just standing there and have everyone collapse at your feet? What a great thing. At least for a little while, anyway. Maybe that's what sparks my Miss Ziegfeld number."

I mentioned to Barbara that I thought her daydream showed strong competitiveness. She selected herself as the most beautiful of her friends, and placed herself strategically at the climax of the presentation, as the sun itself in a universe of beauty. She replied quickly: "Listen, it's my daydream. I'm not coming in second."

She was right, of course. No one ever has to come in second in a daydream. For one supreme moment we can have our way. No one will kick sand in our face. No one will laugh when we sit down at the piano to play. If we want to be beautiful, we can be the most beautiful. Why not?

Barbara had spoken earlier of the carry-over effect of her daydream, that on reentry into the real world she would, for a while, play the role of the Great Beauty. This afterglow phenomenon of daydreaming is a facet of self-image psychology that Dr. Maxwell Maltz describes in his book, *Psycho-Cybernetics* (Prentice-Hall, 1960):

> Experimental and clinical psychologists have proved beyond a shadow of a doubt that the human nervous system cannot tell the difference between an "actual" experience and an experience *imagined vividly and in detail.*

Thus, when we vividly fantasize a desired achievement, event, or state of being, we create an inner climate that heightens our fantasy's potential for coming true. In this way we can actually use fantasy to condition and prepare ourselves for the real-life achievement of our goal. The strong results of much of the new work being done with imagery in therapy make it clear that our fantasies not only reveal our inner selves, but can be used self-consciously to attain goals we set for ourselves. When we "screen" a fantasy, when we imagine something "vividly and in detail," we are, in a way, experiencing it. And, as Dr. Maltz states, "when you 'experience,' something happens inside your nervous system and your midbrain. New 'engrams' and 'neural' patterns are recorded in the gray matter of your brain."

Barbara, when her fantasy was over, felt the afterglow of its effect on her self-image. She could have begun a careful plan to screen that fantasy in glorious color several times a day, and within several weeks, her new showgirl "engrams" securely in place, she might have been ready to tackle an audition for Mr. Ziegfeld. But here is a case where reality could never fulfill a fantasy. The kind of dazzling beauty Ziegfeld traded in, as he put it, the gods bestowed where they would. And where Barbara was, they didn't. The gods did all right by her, indeed. But Mr. Ziegfeld would have passed her by.

Barbara knows that. "Even if I was a roaring beauty, and Mr. Ziegfeld pointed to me and said, 'I'll take that one,' he wouldn't get me," she says. "I don't think the point of the fantasy was ever that I really wanted to be a showgirl. Oh, I'm sure it would be great fun for a short while, especially if

I were twenty again, but in the long run, how boring. What a fragile existence. I think I just wanted to feel like a great beauty for a while. To forget the drill and just get happy. And I did."

Barbara is lucky. She is lovely to look at. Basically she feels content with herself, her life, her looks. Occasionally, when her self-image feels threatened, she calls on a pleasant daydream, gets high, reviews her beauty program, gets on with it.

Most of us have hang-ups about the way we look. Many studies done in recent years on the subject of physical self-image indicate that up to a staggering 90 percent of us think something is wrong with our appearance. Beauty's curse is truly upon us. No wonder the beauty merchants are thriving. And the plastic surgeons. Maxwell Maltz is a plastic surgeon. His work in self-image psychology grew out of his involvement in his profession.

> When I first began the practice of plastic surgery, I was amazed by the dramatic and sudden changes in character and personality which often resulted when a facial defect was corrected. Changing the physical image in many instances appeared to create an entirely new person.

Yet, Dr. Maltz continues in *Psycho-Cybernetics:*

> When a facial disfigurement is corrected by plastic surgery, dramatic psychological changes result only if there is a corresponding correction of the mutilated self-image.

In cases cited by Dr. Maltz, and others described by his colleagues, the conviction that one is no longer ugly was essential to correcting personality problems that accompanied disfigurement.

Many people who seek plastic surgery do not, in the opinion of the professionals they consult, need surgery at all. They have convinced themselves that a disproportionate feature or the natural encroachments of age have compromised their lives, ruined their happiness. And they are miserable. Only the surgeon's knife can save them from the shame of ordinariness, in their opinion.

Our eyes instinctively prize beauty. Our society, and most societies before it have pursued, celebrated, exploited, and foisted it upon us with relentless vigor. When we feel we are not beautiful, we can use our lack of beauty as a scapegoat for our other failings. "If only I were handsomer, I could have gotten the job I wanted, the lover I dreamed of, the popularity I craved." It's so easy to blame our looks for our failings, and to resent the beautiful for the power they acquired so effortlessly.

One night a friend and I invited another couple to dinner. My friend is attractive and accomplished. We prepared the meal together in her home. The other couple were a close friend of mine and his new friend, a quite beautiful woman. The two women had met briefly before at a party, but basically did not know each other.

My companion insisted on preparing the simplest kind of meal, and serving it very casually. I didn't think it particularly odd at the time. But as the evening wore on, she became more and more quiet, distant, disinterested as a hostess, drank a bit too much, and was noticeably cool to the other woman. I became uncomfortable, and lost little time after the other couple had left asking her what her problem was. She was apologetic, and then, with characteristic candor, said: "She is so beautiful, it does me in. She intimidates me completely. I know it's ridiculous, but I can't help it."

I was amazed that the intelligent, responsible, well-adjusted woman I was talking to had so shriveled in the presence of beauty. Yet hers is by no means an uncommon reaction to great beauty in another.

Josephine Huddleston, a beauty expert and columnist of the 1920s, gave us a few choice words on beauty in her book *Secrets of Charm*:

> It is the power that makes most women hate with a burning intensity the woman who has it, for women know its great influence.

A century ago, S. D. Power, in her book *The Ugly Girl Papers*, declared:

> The loveliness of a rival eats into a girl's heart like corrosion; every fair curling hair, every grace of outline, is traced in lines of fire on the mind of the plainer one, and reproduced with microscopic fidelity.

Such bared talons as these could drive a pretty girl to drink. I asked Louise, one of the loveliest women in New York, if she had any fantasies about beauty, what her feelings were about being beautiful, and how she thought others felt toward her.

Louise

"I don't think I have ever had fantasies about *being* beautiful. But I have had fantasies about problems that arose because of my looks. Especially in my early life. Problems in dealing with advances from men. Competitiveness with my mother. *Who* I really was. How people perceived me. [These are related in chapter IV, dealing with fantasies about power].

"I'm sure I have the usual thoughts about how I'm going to look on a given occasion, what I'm going to wear, how people will react to me, and so on. But nothing that really absorbs my imagination in any remarkable way.

"I'm very interested in your question about how I feel others react to my looks, because I do have problems with women from time to time. With some there seems to be a real antagonism, at least on first meeting, as though they were trying to settle something or even some score.

"Some women seem to want to let me know right away they're not impressed. Others want to impress me with some quality or accomplishment of theirs, as though they felt they had to compete. Others want to test me right away, as though they were dying to walk away and say, 'Mmm, she's lovely, but wait till she opens her mouth. Dumb as an ox.'

"This is all rather awkward to talk about, but we're speaking frankly. And I do feel that some people really have a problem with good looks in another. Over the years I've learned to deal with it. I'm not so self-conscious about it anymore. And when I get vibrations of uneasiness in someone, I've learned to cope with it by going out of my way to be pleasant, amusing, whatever.

"It used to make me angry. I felt that I was being singled out for battle, that I had to prove myself in some unusual way to be accepted as a real person. And I worried about whether I seemed to be vain about my looks, and was inviting problems, animosity. It began to give me a complex, as though I had to compensate for something. But I think as time went on, I became more understanding and more tolerant of others *and* myself. And I began to look on it more as a game that I must learn to play.

"One of the worst parts of it was when someone's husband or escort and I would be talking, enjoying ourselves, and the woman would be hovering around positively sending off sparks, sometimes deliberately intruding and breaking up the conversation. Her hostility would give me guilt feelings, and that, in turn, began to affect my enjoyment of being with people. But, as I said before, I think I finally learned to cope with it, and I simply decided it wasn't going to be a problem."

I asked Louise about how she felt about being unusually attractive.

"Of course I love it. It did give me problems. But now it's part of my identity, my feelings about who I am, and I enjoy living with it. Particularly when I see the problems some people seem to have when they feel they are unattractive. Then I feel truly thankful for the ... privilege."

Lola Montez, one of the most celebrated beauties of the nineteenth century, said in her book, *The Arts of Beauty*, published in 1858:

Preach to the contrary as you may, there still stands the eternal fact that the world has yet allowed no higher mission to woman than to be beautiful. . . . All women know that it is beauty, rather than genius, which all generations of men have worshipped in our sex. Can it be wondered at, then, that so much of our attention should be directed to the means of developing and preserving our charms?

No, indeed. This kind of thinking has kept a large chunk of the world's economy afloat for centuries. Cosmetics companies, beauticians, fashion designers, jewelers, hair stylists, and scores of other purveyors of potions, packs, and plumes have for centuries sold us fantasies, most of them expensive, that their creations will favor us where nature would not.

And each time we contemplate the purchase of one of their instant transformations, we fantasize what it will do for us, run a scenario through our heads of how we might just knock them dead in our new tweeds, scent, facelift, golf shirt, diamonds, nose job, boots. And for a moment or two of glory, we stand—unsightly old hair off, slightly new hair on, lips quenched, muscles rippling, blouses plunging, mustaches trimmed, pearls perfectly matched—ready to cloud men's and women's minds with our newly acquired piece of that rock called Beauty.

Primed by our fantasies, we jump, lemminglike, into the sea of fashion, itself a grand conspiracy of fantasy makers. And through the centuries we have splashed about with some remarkable effects. We have painted ourselves blue. Put rings in our noses. Bound our feet into deformity. Pierced our ears. Stretched our necks. Built our biceps. Pumped our breasts full of silicone. And chased our fellow creatures about for their feathers and furs. All in the name of looking good.

But, as S. D. Power, the author of *The Ugly Girl Papers*, put it, "Elegancies of manner are not cultivated without sincere pains." Queen Elizabeth died in a caked mask of powder. The ladies of the court of King Charles II pinned artificial curls to their scalps. The curls were called "heartbreakers." Lola Montez noted:

In Bohemia, I have seen the ladies flock to arsenic springs

and drink the waters, which gave their skins a transparent whiteness; but there is a terrible attachment to this folly.

You bet. The same fate that no doubt attached itself to the beauties of the court of George I, who, Montez noted, "were in the habit of taking minute doses of quicksilver to obtain a white and fair complexion."

So much for the Bohemians and the English. French women seem more sensible. Montez continues:

> I know many fashionable ladies in Paris who used to bind their faces, every night on going to bed, with thin slices of raw beef, which is said to keep the skin from wrinkles, while it gives a youthful freshness and brilliancy to the complexion.

I can see them now, all fresh and brilliant-looking, but practical as ever, serving the beef next noon with *sauce béarnaise* to their unsuspecting husbands.

Men are no better. Roman senators, grown men all, painted curls on their bald pates. Elizabethans packed their groins with codpieces that would have startled any mare. And an early-nineteenth-century men's book called the *Toilette of Health, Beauty, and Fashion* noted that "the ancients considered the hair of the head as the principal ornament of beauty," and quoted Josephus as follows:

> The guards of King Solomon had long hair floating down their shoulders, and every day they powdered their hair with gold spangles, which glistened exceedingly when the sun shown upon them.

Can you imagine what Solomon himself must have looked like? Nothing John Wayne would have cared to impersonate, surely.

Hal

Like Barbara, Hal is in his middle thirties. Also like Barbara, he constructed a fantasy inspired by films, more a coincidence than an illustration that films inspire most fantasies about beauty. His fantasy, or series of fantasies, are of special interest, I think, because of the self-acceptance they encourage.

"When I was a teen-ager, I was not exactly what you'd call a beauty. I was scrawny—it took me longer than most guys to get my full growth—and pretty homely, I guess, and...*shy*. A pretty lethal combination. Girls didn't show any interest in me, and I was really too backward, and, I think, disinterested to go after them.

"Then all at once I fell absolutely head-over-heels in love. The lucky girl was Marilyn Monroe. I had seen a movie called *The Seven Year Itch*, and she really did it to me. It wasn't just that she was so beautiful, which she was; it was more that the character she portrayed—this nice, beautiful girl—said she was tired of handsome lady-killer types making passes at her, that what was really exciting to her were nice, kind, laid-back average guys like Tom Ewell, who played opposite her, and whom I identified with like crazy.

"Well, that did it. The minute I thought that somebody like me could be the love object of someone like Marilyn Monroe I really got interested in the opposite sex—and how. All of a sudden it was 'The Secret Life of Hal Miller.' I had fantasies of making love to her, of her seeking me out, being desperately in love with me. I must have had five thousand different ones about being seen with her—driving around town, eating in restaurants, walking down the street, introducing her as my girl friend to everyone I knew.

"I went to her films over and over again, and pictured myself being the one she was in love with. My friends must have thought I was nuts, because I was probably walking around with my head in the clouds and a silly grin on my face most of the time. It was really very intense—the dreams, the daydreams, the wet dreams, too, no doubt. It was like all at once she was the one who woke me up, got me going. She seemed so beautiful to me.

"My interest in Marilyn lasted a long time. I've thought

about it since, and I'm sure her studio knew what they were doing when they cast her so often as girls who were turned on by ordinary guys. I know in *How to Marry a Millionaire* she wound up with David Wayne, who was broke—and no sex symbol. And in *Some Like It Hot* she wound up with a broke saxophone player. It just seemed that so often the message in her films was that ordinary guys had a chance at something spectacular. It sure hooked me."

And, Hal admitted, it helped him. "I think it helped me a lot to get over my self-consciousness to have fantasies of being loved by someone so beautiful and famous. The problem, of course, came in finding someone to fill her shoes in real life. I did fantasize being irresistible to a few of the class beauties. But they always seemed to be preoccupied with the football players and the class studs. Well, not always. But I guess I was still too shy to give them any kind of a rush.

"But I did start to feel more attractive, and I think just the fact that I was thinking about girls communicated, because I began to notice that some of them had begun to notice me. They would smile and speak, and so on. But I think it was a while before the light dawned on me that, okay, I wasn't handsome, but I was an okay guy, and, therefore, there might be a girl who was not beautiful, but was a super person. And, sure enough, of course, that was true. As a matter of fact, I found the woods full of them.

"So then, I think, as I matured, some nice ordinary girls started showing up in my daydreams, and I got over the need for the beauty thing. I love beauty when I see it, but I don't think I feel hung up about it. I'm still in love with Marilyn, though. And I think in kind of this nice dreamy way I always will be. She was my first."

The Russian poet Yevgeny Yevtushenko in his book *From Desire to Desire* (Doubleday, 1976) wrote:

It's not envy I feel but a kind of pity and revulsion for men who try always to be seen in the company of beautiful women. There is a certain spiritual inferiority in that, a hunger for self-affirmation: "Look at me! I've got a beautiful new woman by my side. I'm worth something."

Well, yes. And no. We've all seen the kind of man Yevtushenko speaks of. The man who must be seen with a beauty, flashing her like a credential. Everything else about him usually contributes in an equally obvious way to a facade of success and power, of having the best, the most, of *holding*. It is a language of illusion, often the only language, disappointingly, that many men, and women, understand and speak.

Yet to judge him too harshly is to discriminate unfairly against the beautiful, who are seldom as shallow as most of us would like to think. And to deny the universality of our love for beauty, an instinctive taste, not an acquired one.

Hal's fantasies of being seen with Marilyn Monroe touch a common fantasy theme. Nearly every man with whom I spoke about beauty related a fantasy of being seen with a beautiful woman, sometimes a famous beauty, sometimes a beautiful woman they had met. If in reality they were in the company of a beautiful woman, they spoke of fantasies they enjoyed of being perceived as a more important, more powerful, more desirable person.

Apparently, if we had our druthers, most of us would rather be beauties. If we're not too concerned one way or another about being beautiful, we would just as soon be seen with a beauty, or ensure that beauty in some shape or form was close at hand. Sometimes beautiful things and beautiful places do the trick.

Lynn

"I have a fantasy of living in the Frick [a great New York mansion filled with the choicest art treasures, now maintained as a museum]. Sometimes, in a moment of longing or boredom or whatever, I close my eyes and imagine myself wandering through those magnificent rooms, pretending it's home. What a perfect setting. Great pictures. Cloisters. Fountains. Marble everywhere. Huge rooms. Long, cool corridors. I fantasize presiding at luscious and elegant parties. [Lynn is regally attractive, and would preside well.]

"I love the idea of its being an extension of myself, the perfect reflection of me, my life, my tastes. I imagine explaining to some distinguished guest or other how I acquired a certain picture, and why it was just the right one for my collection. Ah, if only."

The longing to surround ourselves with beauty has haunted us since we first started sprucing up our caves and hemming up our loincloths. When our natural paradise seemed not enough, we worked up a few treasures of our own—jewels and silks and palaces and works of art. All to please the eye, to try to evoke in ourselves and others the same sense of wonder we feel in the presence of natural perfection. By creating something beautiful on our own, we endeavor to establish our kinship with our creator. Or put one over on him, one of the two. Whatever the reason, the goal is to reproduce in some way the thrill we feel in the presence of a beautiful tree, a sunset, a lovely person.

Though in real life we may be accepting and loving of our less than beautiful physical selves, and our less than perfect friends, in our fantasy world we seldom go out of our way to feature plainness. The artist in us will choose a beautiful face, a fine feature, a perfect setting.

Even though Margaret Mitchell warned us in the first sentence of Gone With the Wind that "Scarlett O'Hara was not beautiful," it is doubtful many of us imagined that spirited creature as less than beautiful. Certainly the producer of the film wouldn't have risked a plain-looking heroine to hold our attention for four hours. And he didn't. And we are grateful for Vivien Leigh's Scarlett, the consummate fantasy heroine come true.

Back to reality. What about us? We may daydream about being beautiful, or bringing beauty into our lives. We may flirt with fashion and self-improvement programs and even raise our self-image. But in matters of physical beauty, the mirror usually has the last word, and all too

often it tells us that Snow White is the real queen. Which is
no reason to feel bad. Or have Snow White put away.

What's to be done then? Be realistic, that's what.
Ziegfeld wasn't wrong when he said beauty cannot be had
for the asking. Where it is held in easy grace, it is a great
gift, and, like Portia's mercy, twice blessed, endowing those
who possess it with true magic, and touching those of us
who behold it with wonder and desire. If it fills us with
jealousy and anger and disappointment and frustration, we
have problems.

Even Lola Montez, who gave beauty a bit more than its
due, graciously admitted:

> The radiance of a charming mind strikes through all de-
> formity of features, and still asserts its sway over the cult
> of the affections.... That chastened and delightful activity
> of the soul, that spiritual energy which gives animation,
> grace and living light to the animal frame, is, after all, the
> real source of beauty.

Let's hear it for Lola. We are all potential beauties after
all. If we believe it. We have all seen the beautiful face
spoiled by arrogance and dullness of spirit. Just as we have
seen the plain face made plain wonderful by a quick and
joyful mind, or a serene and poised soul. These are qualities
that are within our power to cultivate. And if our fantasies
carry us to those most human of all desires for acceptance
and love, not the least of which is self-acceptance and
self-love, they are not fantasies that will lead us astray.
They are fantasies we can make come true, fantasies that
will make us happy when they do.

One of the leading researchers and theorists in the field
of fantasy, Eric Klinger, a professor of psychology at the
University of Minnesota, said in his book *Structure and
Function of Fantasy*:

> Fantasy encompasses a very large share of waking
> awareness.... It thus contributes much of the inner cli-
> mate, much of the mental decor, of being human and of
> being a particular person. It is an important part of the

human being's system for managing large masses of information.... Thus, in this scheme, fantasy is central to human functioning.

Not only are fantasies an important part of our "inner climate," they can be used to change that climate from foul to fair. Our abilities to fantasize and use images creatively have been exploited successfully in new techniques of psychotherapy currently being developed to help us clarify our true identities. Describing some of these techniques, most of them designed to combat negative and erroneous images of ourselves, psychologist Joseph E. Shorr, in his book *Psycho-Imagination Therapy* (Stratton Intercontinental, 1972), concludes: "Liberating a person from an alien identity allows him to be what we are all hopefully striving to be—more human—namely ourselves."

Look in the mirror. A most important part of your life is what you, and therefore others, see reflected there. Do you like what you see? You should. Can you change what you do not like? You can. Can you accept what you cannot change? You must. Few qualities are more attractive than self-acceptance and graceful self-esteem, few more repellent than their opposites.

Those of us locked into loathing and despair of our physical selves should seek help. Professional counseling and therapy can and do change lives. In a few cases, plastic surgery can be the answer. The answer for most of us is some gentle imagining of how we might improve ourselves, and what we will be like when we do, reinforced with a program of action to ease our fantasies into reality.

No less an expert than that legendary trafficker in fantasies of beauty, John Robert Powers, said in his book *Secrets of Charm* (Winston, 1954):

In my years of experience guiding girls and women to their individually chosen goals in every field it is a matter of record that I have never met an unattractive woman—only the one who did not know how to make the most of her natural, attractive self.

Men are no exception to Mr. Powers's rule. Few of us can afford not to make the most of our natural, attractive selves. The marketplace is teeming with books on diet, some of them sensible; on the various benefits of running, jumping, and standing still; on grooming and dressing and all the things that can help us to an improved and approving sense of self. Somewhere in there is a program that can work for you, if a little self-improvement is your game.

And why shouldn't it be? In an era when we are seeking and winning rights and freedoms to be who and what we choose, shouldn't we want to make the most of them, make the most of ourselves? A strong and positive self-image is the best of all possible beginnings. What a relief to walk up to a looking glass, and, to borrow a title from Jean Kerr, (*How I Got To Be Perfect*, Doubleday, 1978) be able to say:

> Mirror, mirror, on the wall,
> I don't want to hear one word out of you.

II. LOVE

He loves,
And she loves,
And they love,
So why can't
You love,
And I love, too?

Ira Gershwin,
"He Loves and She Loves"

Why not? Everybody wants to be in love. It's wonderful, so they say. For light years poets and lyricists have tried to put that certain feeling into words. And we've hummed along, whatever the message. Yes, love is a many-splendored thing. Yes, our love *is* here to stay.

But sometimes love flees, as Yeats would have it, to pace "upon the mountains overhead." And where love goes, our happiness goes, too. Or so we fear.

What is this thing called love? It comes in so many forms. A boy loves his dog. A man loves a good cigar. John loves Mary. Sometimes John loves John. We use the verb *to love* to express a wide range of feelings. The focus here is on those tender feelings two people have for each other, on that happy, sometimes hapless, state we call being "in love."

Everything in our environment conspires to make us feel that love is all—all-important, all-consuming, all around us. And the truth is that when we first felt it deeply ourselves, and didn't fight the feeling, we knew it was something we wanted in our lives. Even when we are fearful of its implications, and find ourselves almost instinctively pulling away from it, other instincts, hopefully healthier, send us back into play.

One of those instincts, or impulses, is the fear of *not* having love. The dread of spending Saturday nights alone has inspired the exchange of a lot of telephone numbers. And our hope, our fantasy that one of those numbers will prove a winner keeps us dialing.

We fantasize what she or he will look like, sound like, be like. When someone of that description walks past us without stopping, we torment ourselves with fantasies of being unattractive, unlovable. When our anxieties and our loneliness become intolerable, a fantasy of a newfound love can offer us valuable respite until the real thing comes along.

Sometimes it's not as desperate as all that. We're just bored. And our busy little minds whip up something tasty just to keep the motor running. We pick someone attractive and interesting and have a go at a love affair. Wonderfully enough, everyone is fair game. It could be our favorite movie idol. The milkman. The girl upstairs in apartment A.

Lynn (chapter I's fantasy mistress of the Frick mansion) is both beautiful and a lover of beauty. She was not at a loss when I asked her for a love fantasy. Not surprisingly, she appears in a goddesslike role, moving serenely through an earthly paradise.

Lynn

"This was a favorite fantasy some years ago when the flower children were blooming everywhere, and we all got into the spirit of things and began posing as these rather romantic waifs, adrift in the cruel world. I had no real love attachment at the time, but was in a highly romantic period in my life, and I envisioned myself as this glorious woodland bride in a wedding of beautiful and free spirits.

"I think the focal point of the fantasy for me was my

lover and husband-to-be. I imagined him very clearly as this godlike creature, classic male perfection, complete with garlands of flowers in his hair. I was in love with his beauty and the purity of his physical image.

"And of course I was aware of my own idealized beauty, and the dazzling effect we both made as these visually perfect lovers. We are in a beautiful parklike setting, under this weeping beech tree [not the least of Lynn's inventions], the world admiring us, subjects of other people's fantasies of love and beauty.

"There is an informal wedding ceremony with poetry and music, everyone saying beautiful things, everyone intoxicated with the magic of the moment. Myself included. I'm very aware of this loving feeling, of having found this perfect lover, of being in love, of being perceived as having found an ideal love."

Lynn's rich imagination never seems to fail her, nor does it fail to place her like a diamond in a Tiffany setting when she wants to feel special. She moves in real life with a grace and poise that would indicate her fantasy life in a very positive way sustains her strongly aesthetic sense of self.

"I love beauty and beautiful things, thinking about them, enjoying them in real life. It helps me keep all the chaos at bay. I'm not oblivious to the ugly and heartbreaking things in life. It's just that I don't choose to dwell on them. I think it can age you, dull your capacity to enjoy all the good things. I think there is much beauty around. And I think it's important to find it and keep it close.

"And one of the most beautiful things to think about *is* love, isn't it? Especially those first feelings that just send you flying."

Karl is much earthier than Lynn. By his own admission, he is less prone to fantasize in his day-to-day life. Yet when he felt the first feelings of love, his daydreams were relentless, turning his mental life into what he called a "Disneyland."

Karl

"For years I'd gotten the hots for different girls, but if I thought...daydreamed about them, it was usually about balling them, or how I'd go about it—where we could go, what she would do, what I would do, how many times we would do it. But that was it. After we did it—mentally, I mean—nothing. I mean, I just didn't think of anything else. But when I met Susan, I began thinking about all kinds of things. And I couldn't believe it.

"We met at college on a blind date, and I liked her right away. And I could tell she liked me. And as usual I was like a walking hard-on for weeks. We weren't making it then, and I thought...daydreamed...a lot about it. But the difference was this time I began daydreaming about a lot of other things. Like where we would go on our next date. What I would wear, or talk about to impress her.

"And for once I just didn't want to snow anybody, you know, about what I wanted to do in life, or what I really thought about something, so I found myself...thinking about myself as she saw me. And that made me think I ought to think more seriously about myself and what I was doing. It wasn't that I didn't have a pretty good idea of who I was and what I was going to do. It just seemed more...real...I seemed more real...when I tried to see myself through her eyes.

"Well, pretty soon I found myself thinking about what my mom and dad would think of her when they met, and my two sisters. And my friends from home. And how a couple of them—one or two girls particularly—might really be surprised, and disappointed maybe. I was working these scenes out in my head like crazy. And it was great because everybody liked Susan.

"The next thing I knew I was doing things like writing her name down with my last name, you know, like Mrs. Susan Johnson. Susan Taylor Johnson. Susan and Karl Johnson. Karl and Susan Johnson. Just to see what it would look like. So obviously I was thinking about something a little heavier than just making out.

"*Then* I started looking at those home magazines that illustrate all kinds of houses, with the plans and everything. I bought a few and spent hours thinking about which one I liked best, and how I could get it built. Then I began thinking about children—how many, what they'd look like, buying toys, you name it. I tell you it was a whole thing."

I asked Karl if before he met Susan he'd had thoughts or general ideas about when or even if he might get married, and how getting married would fit in with the kind of life he hoped to lead.

"Oh, I think I always had in the back of my mind I'd get married and do the whole thing. My folks have a good marriage, I think, and most of my family are...the marrying kind, I guess you could say. There have been some divorces, but by and large, everybody gets married. And I've always pretty much bought the package. I mean, I always figured I'd go into business, get married, have a family. The usual thing."

He reaffirmed that, while he had had some previous fantasies about love relationships and being married, it wasn't until he met Susan that his "love dreams" became a repeated and intense activity.

"It got really funny at one point. We'd be going out, and talking and necking and so on, and I'd never let on about what I had been thinking—about the houses and meeting my folks and the rest. I was daydreaming a lot about going to bed with her, and we still weren't at the point where we could talk about *that*—other than the usual "not yet" routine. And I kept thinking, wouldn't it bowl her over to know I was thinking about something other than just balling. And then, of course, pretty soon I knew I really cared a lot about her, and I was in love, I guess. And I don't think you can really hide that, or keep it from somebody. It just comes through.

"So I had to tell her, and I did, and it was great. Because she said she loved me, too. We didn't talk about getting married right away. But pretty soon we both started hinting about it, and talking a lot about people who were getting married and getting divorced and why, and so on. And then one day I told her I wanted to marry her and she said yes and that was that.

"I think we kind of daydreamed together after that. I mean, really, we'd both sit there and get spaced out about how we saw things, how we'd do this, how we'd do that. And I remember running things through my head by myself about living with her and what our life would be like. But nothing quite like that first time I really started thinking about her. I'll never forget what that was like. It was Disneyland. I'm not kidding."

Karl admitted to some vague thoughts about falling in love, getting married, going into business, of "buying the whole package." But in college his interests revolved primarily around scores and scoring until he met Susan. In *Structure and Function of Fantasy*, Eric Klinger writes: "Both play and fantasy reflect current focal concerns of the individual—unresolved current problems, unfinished tasks, role conflicts . . . as well as the challenges of identity and commitment posed by the individual's social relationships."

When Karl daydreamed about Susan and their possible relationship, he not only renewed and prolonged the sexual excitement he felt when he was with her, he also explored the extent of the role she might play in his life. Fantasizing helped him to envision and evaluate the impact of her arrival in his world. And as his feelings toward her deepened and became more involved, his daydreams helped him cope with the implications of those feelings, helped him prepare for his real life with Susan.

"Happy people never make fantasies, only unsatisfied ones do." No less a student of the mind than Sigmund Freud said that decades ago. If only he had met Karl. And if only he could have devoted more of his time to the investigation of *day*dreams.

"Now psychologists have learned from clinical and

experimental research that daydreams are normal to all active minds," says Jerome Singer, a professor of psychology at Yale University and a leading figure in the study of daydreams. "They are a very real part of our growth and self-development." Through them we can "modify a dull situation, plan for the future, try out new ways of relating to people around us." (*Readers Digest*, June 1975.)

Most psychologists today agree that Freud's opinion that only unsatisfied people daydream is at best only partially true. "Happy" people make fantasies as readily as "unsatisfied" people do. And through fantasy both varieties cope with their feelings, their hopes, their anxieties and fears about many things, including, and especially, about love, one of the most gratifying ways of "relating to people around us."

Karl's feelings for Susan followed a normal pattern of attraction, and his fantasies helped him lay the groundwork for a reasonably typical marriage-and-family lifestyle.

Sometimes we have loving feelings that bewilder us, that we find difficult or impossible to accept—often because they are not socially acceptable. And through our fantasies we attempt to cope with the anxieties and fears that those feelings cause.

Mark

"I think it was in my fantasy life that I first became acquainted with my homosexuality. From as early as I can remember, all of my loving and sexual feelings, and all of my good and bad responses to them, showed up in my daydreams. When I learned to be ashamed of my feelings, my fantasies were dominated by fear—fear of being found out, fear of being exposed, laughed at. If there was someone I was attracted to, I would imagine all kinds of negative responses to any advances I might make.

"All of this served, of course, to keep the closet door locked tight. I mean the fantasies of punishment and scorn no doubt helped keep me in line—and in migraine headaches.

"I had the usual sort of homosexual experiences as a young boy—a little mild playing around—but had not felt guilty or troubled about it. Probably because there were enough others who indulged that it didn't make me feel it was wrong, or anything to worry about.

"Then high school came along, and we all began talking about sex openly—not just groping around under the sheets. Words like *queer* and *fairy* and *homo* came into the vocabulary pretty quickly, and it became very obvious you had to . . . choose sides. There were a couple of older guys in the school who had the reputation of indulging—a few girls, too—and the warning came loud and clear: *don't* unless you want to become a walking joke.

"Well the choice wasn't too difficult. And at first I didn't have any real problems with it. I liked girls, and had fun dating and necking, even considered myself 'going steady' a few times, and felt good about it.

"But I was aware of some special feelings, some crushes I had on some of the upperclassmen, and even some guys in my class. And the fantasies that I had began to be more sexual in tone than those about the girls I knew and liked.

"I couldn't talk about it with anyone, but somewhere along the line I picked up an idea or two that those kinds of feelings were not necessarily to worry about, that adolescents often had crushes on others of the same sex—like kids for their camp counselors—and that it all straightened itself out in time.

"At that age, by early high school, there was no sexual intimacy with my friends, or even any hint of it. Any admission of homosexual feelings would be asking for big trouble. Overnight the game was *girls*, and everybody joined the team.

"So there were no more experiences of any sort like the ones I had had at eleven or twelve. But the love fantasies for some of the boys I knew grew and grew. They would involve secretive meetings, having sex—probably masturbating each other—vowing secrecy and carrying around these intense loving feelings, very sexual.

"Sooner or later I got into fantasizing myself as a girl, as someone who could openly attract and date and be the steady playmate of the boy I wanted. And sometimes I would fantasize the boy as a girl, and do the whole thing in reverse.

"But at the same time I *also* had fantasies of going out with girls, of having a special girl friend, or being thought of as a regular guy. I know I thought someday I would really fall in love with a girl, forget all the guy stuff, get married, have children, do the normal thing.

"College was pretty much a continuation of the same. No experiences. Crushes on guys. Lots of big talk about 'queers.' Dating girls. Some heavy necking, but no sex with them. Some awareness of playing a game. And the beginnings of some angry feelings about being different, about being some lower species.

"I had opportunities for sex with men. I knew where to get it, if I wanted it, with certain of the guys on campus. But I was too scared—of what others would think if they found out, of what I would think if it happened.

"I had gone away to college out in the Midwest, and when I came back to the city, I lived a while with my folks. But then in a few months, I got a job and got my own apartment in Manhattan. I started dating some girls I knew from school, but nothing serious developed. And I began to think, 'I've got to get something on, one way or the other.' I had heard about some gay bars and other places you could meet gay guys, and I thought, 'I have to try it.' And I did. And from the very first moment I knew it was going to happen to me, I loved it.

"Until the next morning when all the guilt and confusion set in, and I was one miserable man. 'What's happening here? I can't accept this. What will people think?' I had agonizing fantasies of how my parents would react if they found out. Scenes of shock and rejection. Of what my friends would think. Scorn. Laughter. Put-downs. Then I would swear off, and try to fantasize finding the right girl and getting over it all. But in a few days I'd be over that part of it, and back looking for more.

"For a long time I continued to move in both worlds, to think of myself as AC-DC. I allowed myself to be seduced by girls a few times and enjoyed it. And I seduced a few myself, and enjoyed that. But what was missing was that big emotional flash I felt when I was with a man. It just never happened with girls, though I was capable of very affectionate feelings for them, and got through the sex part just fine. With flying colors, as a matter of fact.

"I think the thing that kept me trying for so long with girls, besides the big fear of being exposed as a homosexual, was that down deep I thought of myself as a family man. I love children. I always wanted to have about ten. I remember once when I was in college I had a very vivid dream about becoming a father—holding the baby, feeling very special, so wonderful, so proud. And I remember for days feeling relieved, that it was a sign of some sort that everything would be all right, that I would straighten out. And I had a lot of fantasies about which of the girls I was dating would be the mother.

"And I've had many daydreams of myself in the role of father, everything from toys and zoos to helping with the homework. One more dream, not daydream, I'll tell you about. As time went along, and I guess the thought of ten children seemed to be stretching it, I dreamed of fathering triplets—a complete family in one fell swoop! And that dream worked on me like the first one—very reassuring. There was hope. And my image of myself as a potential father kept on surviving.

"But I could never really make the whole thing add up. I think the biggest stumbling block of all is that it seemed so obviously unfair to enter a heterosexual marriage harboring such strong homosexual tendencies. It would certainly be unfair to the woman involved, unfair to the children you might have, if it didn't work out. I have seen too many instances where it didn't work out, and people got hurt, sometimes badly.

"Back to the fantasies. I still have very strong ones about finding a relationship with a man I can feel good about, one that might be permanent . . . committed. I can't seem to find a relationship that really works. But the fantasy usually involves some kind of special setting—away from everything, where we can be together without being thought of as freaks.

"Sometimes I have fantasies of just coming out and the hell with it and who cares, and accepting the whole thing and making the best of it. And I've pictured confrontations with my family and friends—and at work. I think now if I found the right person I would do just that, and get it all over with. The climate is much better for that approach now."

I asked Mark if he had ever had any kind of counseling to help him in any way sort out his feelings and, to use his earlier expression, "take a side."

"Ten years ago I did, and the man I worked with helped me see the conflict more clearly. I had been feeling very anxious and frustrated about my ambivalence—I was going into my mid twenties, and no clear path was emerging.

"He helped me think of myself as a good person with special feelings, not as a freak. But I think it was too early for me to respond well to therapy. Even though I was worried about myself, I was having fun. And there still seemed to be time to grow out of it. Despite all my conflicts, my ego has always been strong. Eventually I drifted away from seeing him.

"I've heard of various programs of using positive images, fantasies, of heterosexual experiences, negative ones of homosexual experiences to help reorient your sexual feelings. And I did try it on my own some years back. Which is probably not a good idea. It didn't do much for me. At the point I tried it, it was like asking the Hudson to flow backwards.

"Some time I may try therapy again. It might help now, who knows? I think the truth of it all is that I would love to have a wife and family, but not unless I was sure I could give up the homosexual part of me. I would just feel too vulnerable. And I'm afraid I could never be sure.

"If I had my choice I would like to have been resoundingly heterosexual. But my life hasn't been all that painful. And I don't really regret my homosexual experiences. They've been too good. And, believe it or not, I haven't given up hope yet that I'll work it all out and end up an old family man. I would have had the best of both worlds. Maybe that's what keeps my fantasies going. I want everything."

Mark's fantasies helped him sort his way through his anxieties about his sexuality, helped him make choices about them, and helped him construct conflicting images of himself as both an active homosexual and a family man, incompatible roles in real life, in his view.

As yet, the homosexual condition is largely an unknown. Many theories and therapies exist. But nothing definitive has yet emerged. Except society's long-entrenched position that homosexual relations are bad form at best; at worst bad news for everyone concerned.

To be by nature in conflict with society is a tough one, and those of us caught up in it might be entitled to every kind of paranoid fantasy. Mark's position is perhaps somewhat easier than some with homosexual preferences. He has sexual feelings for women, too, and seems equally capable of moving in heterosexual and homosexual worlds. His desires to be a family man are not necessarily unrealistic, more perhaps overshadowed by the strength of his homosexual orientation, which he feels would be destructive to any family life he might undertake.

His awareness of his feelings, his choices, his preferences were brought more sharply into focus by his daydreams. Particularly in the early years, when there was no one with whom he could discuss his feelings, his fantasies became a theater of the mind, on whose stage he could dramatize both the fulfillment of his feelings and the anger, conflict, and hope he felt about his condition.

We can fantasize going along *with* society, too,

particularly when all the promised rewards are so attractive, and the socially approved goal is just our cup of tea.

Kathleen

"I remember I was crazy about dolls when I was a little girl. I played a lot with them, especially when I was with friends. We'd have parties with them, work up little plays. And we changed their clothes a lot. My grandmother really could sew, and she'd make up all kinds of outfits. Including wedding gowns. I think every one of my dolls had a wedding gown.

"I remember going to a lot of weddings when I was young. I come from a big family, and I had ... *have* ... a lot of cousins, and young aunts and uncles, and so on, and it seemed like somebody was always getting married. A couple of times I was a flower girl.

"I loved getting all dressed up and being the center of attention. And I remember having weddings with our dolls, and the family would get a big kick out of it. And somebody would always make some comment about how, before I knew it, I'd be doing it for real, you know.

"And sure enough, all of a sudden there I was in my teens, talking a lot about getting married with my friends, and daydreaming my head off about it. The conversation would always edge around sex, you know, and how far to go and so on, but an awful lot of talk was about weddings. Wedding dresses. Wedding veils. Who would be bridesmaid for who. Where the reception would be. Who would come. Who we wouldn't ask.

"Then I remember more and more having a very definite daydream, where I would see myself coming down the aisle, having people turning to look at me through the candles and the flowers at the end of the pew, and looking down to where the bridegroom stood there at the altar.

"That would be funny, because the chances were there'd be a different person standing there every time, depending

on who I thought was cute that week. I do remember—
actually I still do it sometimes—what a high I got from
pretending to be a bride. I remember one period in
particular when The Carpenters recorded, 'Love, Look at
the Two of Us' ["For All We Know" is the actual title], and
people were using it as processional music at weddings. I
had been to one where they used it, and it really knocked
me out. Every time I'd hear it I'd have this big thing going
on in my head about being a bride. It gave me a wonderful
feeling."

I asked Kathleen how much she thought about the other
person waiting at the altar, whether or not loving feelings
were part of her daydreams. She continued:

"Yes, sometimes. If I was in the middle of a crush on
someone, I guess. But I think that I was much more into
being a bride rather than really getting married. Here it is,
my big moment, and all that. In the period when I really
daydreamed like this, I don't think I was even dating
anyone, other than just hanging around with a group. But I
did think about love—and sex. It was probably all blurred
together.

"I'll tell you something. I've always been very romantic-
minded. Just being near somebody I like, touching them,
spending time with them was always the most important
thing. I never really fantasized about the sex part too
much. When it did come along, it was like just a really
terrific part of being together, really close, to someone
I . . . *loved*.

"I did fantasize about *that* . . . love, I mean. When I did get
married, I thought about all the time we would have
together, the things we could do together. And I'll tell you
it's been a lot like I thought it would. It's been about a year
and a half now since we got married and so far, so good.
Great, as a matter of fact."

I asked Kathleen about her wedding.

"Well, it was just like all the ones I went to as a little girl.
And a lot like the ones I had thought about. But I'll tell you
honestly, it got to be a drill. And there were moments when
I was thinking this whole business is kind of nutty . . .

unreal. Between setting dates, and looking at six-hundred-dollar dresses and two-hundred-dollar veils, and so much per person for a reception, and so much for this, and so much for that, and who's coming, and what we ought to spend, I started thinking, 'No way I'm going to make it through this.'

"But Dad and Mom were great. They liked Jerry a lot, and were really glad we were getting married. Somehow we worked it all out, kept it a nice simple church wedding with a reception in the church hall, and it all went one-two-three. What was really strange was that I really got cool as a cucumber. I think I was so afraid it was going to be a drill, that I laid *way* back.

"That worked until the minute I saw Dad in his tux and he saw me in my wedding dress, and that did it. We both got really teary-eyed—my mother, too—but we got into the car and on the way to the church I got high as a kite. I mean, here it was—all real. Complete with the wedding dress my grandmother had made.

"The next thing I knew I heard the wedding music, and looked into the church with all the candles lit, and saw Jerry, and it was all so beautiful, and I started with the tears—and shaking. It's just I was so moved. I can't tell you. I was so thrilled. Then I saw Jerry smiling, and I saw that people had begun to look around to see me, and I straightened up, and it all went just great."

As Kathleen first spoke, I thought I was hearing the living, breathing testament of someone so severely socially conditioned she might commit mayhem for a handful of orange blossoms. But as she continued to talk, and we later reflected on her fantasies, she seemed very much the well-adjusted young woman who had met someone she liked, married him, and settled down. Like Karl, perhaps, she "bought the package," and, when all the elements fell into place, put it all together, and headed out for happily-ever-after.

Marriage has been working for us for aeons. And weddings over the centuries have become showpieces of our culture, replete with beautiful costumes and settings,

touching words, explosions of well-wishing and revelry—
the stuff of dreams and fantasies. There we are, producing
and starring in our own film, cast with those we love,
flocked to by friendly faces bearing silver-plated oyster
forks.

Daydreams can and do feature the attainment of socially
acceptable, socially prized goals. But the social pressures to
get married, get smart, get rich, and get on with it
sometimes seem relentless. At best they give us something
to shoot for. At worst, something to shoot at, when their
pursuit causes frustration and unhappiness, and we
discover we may have pursued an illusion.

Kathleen played wedding with her dolls in wedding
dresses her grandmother had sewn. She had been taken to
weddings as a young girl, been a flower girl, been told she
would be a bride soon enough, been a bridesmaid,
fantasized being a bride, and finally made it, just under the
line, a few months before she was twenty-one. One could
have forgiven her for grabbing just about anyone and
dashing for the finish line. But she didn't.

"I know what you're saying about illusions," Kathleen
continued, "or at least I think I do. And I'll admit I probably
would feel really out of it if I never got married. I mean, I
really wanted to fall in love and get married very much. I
always thought it would be part of my life. But I didn't
marry Jerry just to . . . get myself off the market, you know.
Or because I thought I had to get married just to please
everybody. We met, got along really well, and in a few
months we knew, and in about six months we got married.

"I'll tell you something. My mother was terrific when
we'd talk about what being married was all about, so maybe
that steered me away from wrong ideas about it. She
wasn't too great about the sex part. I mean she let it be
known she didn't approve of anything before marriage.
Period. So she wasn't exactly the kind of mother you could
go to to help you get on the pill. So between that and being
scared to death of getting pregnant, and scared to death of
getting VD, which was really going around a lot when I was
in high school, I just didn't . . . you know . . . mess around.

But anyway, she always said you have to work at marriage. It wasn't just making love and having a good time. And I began paying attention to how they treated each other— Mom and Dad—and made decisions together, things like that. How they could get mad, and then talk it out and get over it. There was a lot of talking."

We *make* love. Make it happen. Make it last. Day by day. Love doesn't just fly in, wave its wand, and make everything taste good. We make marriages, too. Day by day. Working. Caring. Seeing it through.

When love does happen to us, works for us, endures, many of our fantasies revolve around the anticipated pleasures of sharing our experiences and thoughts with our lover. "I wonder how he'll take it?" "Oh, will she get a kick out of this." In anticipating, visualizing the reactions of another who is close to us, our own feelings are heightened, our potential pleasure can be doubled, our pain intensified.

Mary Ann and Doug

"Whenever the hassle at work is too much for me— everything is going wrong, and I'm beginning to literally stew—I just think about getting home, walking in the door, and sitting down with Doug. Immediately I get the feeling that everything's going to be okay. I get this mental picture of him. I see his reassuring reactions to my problems. I know he'll come up with something that will make me feel a lot better.

"Even if there are no specific problems, maybe I'm just bored to tears with what I'm doing, or just don't want to do it, I focus on that moment of seeing Doug, maybe having a cocktail, fixing dinner, chatting with him. And everything starts to feel right to me."

Mary Ann and Doug are over forty, have separate careers, and have had a happy and comfortable marriage for years. "I have similar thoughts about Mary Ann," Doug said. "Whether it's buying something for her, and imagining how she'll look in it. Or maybe telling her some piece of news, or sharing some thought with her and imagining how she'll react. It's almost automatic with me, and almost always pleasurable.

"If something negative happens, something that I know will upset her or make her worry, I imagine how she will take it, and I'll try out different ways of breaking it to her to minimize her reaction."

"I think there are times," Mary Ann added, "that before I've worked something through, if I have a problem, I think of Doug's input in coping with it, and try to come up with a solution that would make sense to him as well as to me."

"There are times," Doug concluded, "that I think of Mary Ann's reaction before I do something, and wind up not doing it. Not always, but sometimes," he laughed.

Doug and Mary Ann are companions in their fantasies as well as in the real world. Karl's daydreams about love were pretty much X-rated adventure films until he met Susan and his scripts started running to domestic comedy. Kathleen fantasized weddings, and one day found herself a bride, in love with someone who loved her. Life is not always so kind to us. The opportunity to love doesn't always present itself when we're ready for it. Sometimes when it does, we're not ready, and it's only later, often with regret, that we sense a missed cue. So much, of course, depends on our personal qualities and the choices we make about our lives.

Some of us blissfully undertake, or stumble through, a variety of love experiences. Some of us retreat, sometimes gracefully, from love's pleasures and demands, devoting our energies to the pursuit of power, glory, love of God, love of family, devotion to causes, institutions, abstractions, all of which can offer formidable rewards. Formidable frustrations, too, if in the midst of our noble or ignoble efforts, we find ourselves daydreaming of that loving companion we promised ourselves in some tomorrow.

"When a person's daydreams run completely counter to

their life experience, that person may be overlooking an important part of his or her essential nature," Jerome Singer said in a recent article in *Vogue* (November 1976). Daydreams can offer us important cues to unfulfilled needs communicated by our deepest selves. If visions of someone special dance through your head at ever-increasing intervals, it could be time to get out the dancing shoes and give someone a break.

Afraid to try? Too shy? Tired of being rejected? Tired of the same old thing, of the people you like not liking you? Afraid someone will think you're on the loose and on the make? Well, stay home, then. See if your daydreams substitute for the real thing. They can't. They don't. And they never will. They can do much for you. But when the sun goes down, they are cold comfort.

If your daydreams drift toward scenes with a lover, be kind to yourself. No matter what your past mistakes, failures, regrets, try again and keep trying. The real you is telling you something important. As Walt Whitman put it, "Now, Voyager, sail thou forth to seek and find." And when you find, be good to yourself, and to your new friend.

Joan

"Of all the things that brought us down, I blame my jealousy. *Why* I was so jealous I'm tracking down now with Dr. Smith [her analyst]. But while we were married I just couldn't handle it, or myself, really, for that matter. Bob was a terribly attractive man. He liked women, and it showed. Not that he made passes, at least not to my knowledge. But he was one of those men that women just gravitate to, smiling, teasing, the rest. And it drove me insane.

"He knew of my feelings, and for a long time I think he really tried to avoid incidents that might get me going. And when we talked about it, I think we just glossed it over with some platitude or other that I was just the jealous type, and that we'd just live with it and not let it spoil anything. And he assured me time and again there were no real grounds for jealousy.

"I remember absolutely torturing myself with fantasies of where he was and what he was doing. I pictured him seducing or being seduced by everybody in our group, by his secretary or someone he worked with. You name it. I mean, how could anybody be so insecure, or want to hurt themselves so much?

"Now that I can see the depth of the problem, it all seems so terribly silly. But then, all I could see was how much I loved him, and how desperately afraid I was that someone else would get him away from me. And I mean desperate. And no matter how I tried to cover up the mania, it showed. And month by month it brought out more and more antagonisms, and in the end just blew us apart."

If love is important to us, fear of losing love can make us more wretched than not having it to begin with. Joan is in her early forties, is divorced after eighteen years of marriage, raising three children, and working as an executive secretary. She has undergone analysis and therapy. Neither she nor her husband have remarried after two years. They date others, and see each other occasionally, "on a very reserved, but friendly basis."

The story of her marriage and its breakup is a long and interesting one, best discussed by a trained analyst and commentator. But it is interesting here in the sense that Joan used daydreams, or found herself swept up into fantasizing, to aid and abet the destructive energies of her jealousy, itself the product of her insecurities and inabilities to find her balance in a love relationship.

"He would be barely out the door, and my mind would start twisting and turning. I'd picture him using a friend's apartment to meet his secretary, driving to a friend's house while her husband was out of town. In the end I'd actually start phoning around with some excuse or other to check up on him.... Ghastly. And the truth is, I really loved him. And he loved me.... Until I made it impossible."

Again, what is love? Certainly trust must be part of it.

But first and foremost it appears that it is a prerequisite of love that we love ourselves first, that we consider ourselves worthy of another's love. It's important, too, that we enter into a loving relationship feeling free to be ourselves, and expect our loved ones to be nothing other than themselves, to require of them no special concessions to merit our love. In this simple, mutual acceptance, "there are no gimmicks to your giving," says psychologist Wayne Dyer in *Your Erroneous Zones* (Funk & Wagnall's, 1976). "You're not doing it for the thanks or the payoffs but because of the genuine pleasure you get from being a helper or a lover."

This kind of love seldom floats through our fantasies, certainly not so often as the fleeting moment of passion so dear to our home screens. But it is the kind that can make lovemaking an art, and each of us who gives it our best a fellow artist.

Most of us are a bit self-concerned at heart in that we want to be loved, expect to be loved as part of the good life we envision for ourselves. Yet if we were to spend more time building in our minds an image of ourselves as lovers, as givers of attention, comfort, solace, inspiration, amusement, rather than as loved ones, we might build for ourselves a life where love was always close at hand.

So much of what we do, and how we handle what happens to us, flows out of the image we construct of ourselves in our heads. Our fantasies not only reflect and dwell upon our desires and problems, they create the climate through which those desires are achieved, those problems are solved.

Psychologists working in the fields of imagery and self-image psychology have achieved remarkable results in programs designed to break down negative self-images that produce pain and confusion in our lives, and to replace them with those more likely to fulfill our healthiest wishes.

If we build images of ourselves as strong, consistent givers of love and invest ourselves not in a thoughtless taker of love, but another strong and confident giver, we are likely to find that love truly can be a many-splendored thing, a happy sharing of the give and take of loving gestures, a joyful bond of mutual acceptance.

As the Unicorn said to Alice:

> Well, now that we have seen each other,
> if you believe in me, I'll believe in you.
> Is that a bargain?

The best.

III. SEX

Wild nights! Wild nights!
Were I with thee,
Wild nights should be
Our luxury!

Emily Dickinson
"Wild Nights"

We'll never know how luxuriously Emily Dickinson furnished her vision of wild nights. Reading these lines, it's possible to guess that the reclusive Amherst poet was no stranger to fantasies of the flesh. Daydreams with sexual themes are staples of the active imagination. Indeed, they can be the most insistent, elaborate, and bizarre of our daydreams.

In England several years ago, Edward Thorne undertook "a number of exploratory conversations with normal people about what they imagine in the way of erotica," which he reported in his book *Your Erotic Fantasies* (Neville Spearman, 1971). What he reported would indicate that many of us are highly accomplished pornographers. Or, as he put it, "After reading the transcripts of interviews that were undertaken for this survey, one could never take a bus-queue of people at their face value again."

When I mentioned to friends and associates that I was working on a book about daydreams and fantasies, eyes rolled, grins widened, and a surprising number of people turned tease immediately with an "Oh, what I could tell you." Some of them did tell me, with wonderful combinations of relief, abandon, confession, daring, wonderment, aplomb. Our growing ability to share our thoughts and feelings about sex with reasonable candor is one of the few anxiety-reducing things that has happened to us in this century.

Of course, some of us are still terribly anxious about sex, don't like to talk about it, and are not at ease when others do. As President Carter found out. In the famous interview he gave *Playboy* magazine as a presidential candidate in 1976, he confessed: "I've looked on a lot of women with lust. I've committed adultery in my heart many times."

This confession disheartened more than a few of Mr. Carter's supporters, and almost cost him the election. Apparently we're still not ready to hear about some kinds of fantasies from our presidents-to-be. Chickens in pots, yes. Sex, no.

Yet it's comforting to think that poets and presidents might share our enthusiasm for daydreaming about sex. And it's reassuring to know that recent studies and research have shown that most of us have sexual fantasies, that they are characteristic of the healthy, creative adult, and that they can enhance our sexual relationships with their special power to arouse and stimulate sexual desire.

Our sexuality, urged on by a culture that uses sex lavishly to spread its influence, prompts in us a broad range of responses from curiosity and desire to anxiety and fear. In our attempts to handle the emotions they stir, we create some of our most engaging fantasies. And why not? In our daydreams the sky is the limit. Everyone is fair game. Anything goes.

Tom

"I had a fraternity brother and close friend in college who was a riot, a long, lanky cowboy-type from Montana. His family had a ranch out there and I think were well off, because he always seemed to have plenty of money, and he drove a big red Oldsmobile convertible.

"He was always making out like a bandit. I don't know how he did it, but he always had girls crawling all over him. I mean, I was in awe of him. I think of all the people I knew in those days he was the one I envied most.

"Well, one spring night he just disappeared off campus. We bunked together so I knew right away he must have been up to something. And I didn't see him until the next night, when he walked into the fraternity house looking kind of glazed and said he was just going to clean up and grab a change of clothes and take off again.

"I couldn't pry out of him what was going on. All he would say was, 'You won't believe what's happening,' and 'I'll be back in a couple of days and tell you all about it.' Well, he wouldn't say much more, and he left. And I remember being ticked off as hell.

"Then, sure enough, in a couple of days he came back, looking more spaced out than ever. And then he told me these stories that have stuck in my fantasy world ever since. And that's been twenty years ago.

"Basically what happened was, he was picked up at a local hangout by these two girls who were apparently just driving through the countryside picking up guys, taking them to their motel and shacking up with them for a few days. Two girls. Two beauties, to hear him tell it, just out spreading the good news state to state. He said they were on a big coast-to-coast joyride with plenty of money and a very hearty appetite for college boys.

"Well, here I was, a college boy in *need*. And I was so damned mad at him for not letting me in on the fun I almost punched him out. He kept saying what a kick it was to be alone with two girls. Especially those two. Everything in the book, apparently. Everything you'd see today in the porno palaces, but in those days it really sounded off the wall.

"I must have bitched so much that he took pity on me and said they had told him they would be coming back through in a few days—they were off giving someone else a break up the road somewhere—and he'd try to get me in on the party, or send me in for relief or something.

"Well, that really got me going. I thought and thought about all the things he had told me that they had done and done and done, and I was a basket case for days just dreaming about my big chance. Which never happened, because they never called. I think we hung around the telephone for days waiting for their call. It's a wonder we didn't flunk something. But no luck. And no phone call.

"Once I got that picture in my head, it just never left me. Whenever I thought about sex, which was just about every other minute in those days, I thought about myself going through all those wonderful exercises with those two girls. And I kept pumping Phil—my friend—for all the details of what the girls looked like, what they said to him while they were doing it—everything. They were both brunettes, I remember that.

"And the more I got down the details, the more elaborate I made my daydreams. To this day if I see two cute gals in a car, or sometimes if I even pass a motel I'll think about that incident and the daydreams. And being with two girls is still just about my favorite daydream about sex. I'll change it around from time to time to suit myself—change the faces and so on—but it all goes back to Phil and his damned red convertible and those little sweethearts.

"I wish I could tell you it finally happened to me in real life—going to bed with two girls—but it never did. As far as threesomes go, I'm still a virgin. Do you think there's still hope?"

We agreed there's always hope. I asked Phil if the opportunity presented itself tomorrow, would he follow those two brunettes to their motel. His first reaction was a quick "Are you kidding?" But, reflecting a bit, he said, "You know, I don't know how I would act in reality at this point. Put it this way: I wouldn't go looking for them. Often in my daydream they flaunt themselves at me, picking *me* out for fun and games. And I, of course, never resist.

"But I think the chances for that happening for real are

zilch at this point in my life. I'm not this nice ripe college boy anymore. And the chances of finding two girls on the prowl who aren't hookers would be out of sight, anyway. And the thought of paying for it really spoils the fun of it.

"I think that was one of those once-in-a-lifetime things that comes very close to you, gets you all excited, then never happens, but leaves you with the sweet and the sour of it forever. One great moment of lust—or almost lust—*bronzed*.

"Truth and honesty, I haven't played around since I've been married. The thought has occurred to me, and I've had opportunities many times. But I just never did. It's not so much that I wouldn't *do that* to Jean. I think it's more that I wouldn't want to do it to *my* feelings about us, which have been great all these years. Why play around with that?

"So I think about sex with others—the two-girl thing is really the only one that recurs noticeably—but I don't think about doing it for real."

As we talked further, we considered some of the possible motivations and payoffs for Tom's daydreams. Certainly they put him in touch with an intensely erotic moment from the past that still could serve him well as sexual inspiration. And it was a potent stimulant for the ego: The girls selected Tom, found him irresistible. And Tom made sure their confidence was not misplaced. "Just call me Tom the Great Satisfier. Not just one, but *two*, mind you," he laughed.

"I think it just shores up my macho every now and then," he continued. "I mean it *has* to. There are times I have this image of myself leaving the sack with these two totally exhausted females collapsed there on the sheets.

"One more thing makes it work just right for me. Not only does it make me feel like superman, it avoids commitment problems. No worries about 'Who is this that I'm in bed with? What does it mean?' With two of them there are no real feelings of *involvement* to complicate things. Just lust in the dust, a perfect little adventure."

Tom's favorite fantasy was inspired by a real incident in

his early life. Pat's was first inspired by a feeling of being vulnerable, that "anything could happen," and she allowed it to happen in this richly detailed scenario that neatly avoids too many details of actual physical contact.

Pat

"I'm in my office working late. Everyone else has gone home for the night. It is dark out, and I can look out my window and see the lights on in the buildings across the street. It's summer. I have something kind of loose and flimsy on. The air conditioning has gone off, and it's very quiet. I hear footsteps, kind of heavy, and a jingling sound. It startles me at first, then I remember that it must be time for the night watchman to be making his rounds. I hear him fiddling with the light switches, and see some of the main lighting outside in the office area go out. The footsteps come closer and suddenly this tall figure looms into view at my door.

"The guard has on some kind of short-sleeved summer uniform, has a holster with a gun in it, and a big bunch of keys hanging from his belt. And he's not the usual night watchman. He's someone I recognize who used to work in the mailroom. Well, we're both startled. He says he didn't know anyone was still here. And I say I didn't expect to see him here as a watchman. He explains that he's working now as a watchman so that he can go to classes during the day. So obviously he's college age, and need I mention, wildly attractive. And in real life I had seen him often before. We'd exchanged glances a few times, and I must say I had thought to myself, 'Mmm, anytime you're ready.' That sounds awful, but I did think it.

"Well, he kind of lingers a little, and I notice he's looking me over pretty closely, and he tries to make a little conversation about my working late. I try to keep it light, and act as though I'm just looking up from my work, and about to get back to it. But he talks on in a very conversational way, like we had just met at a dance or something.

"Then I begin to get a little nervous and excited, and I think he sees it. He begins with the eyes again, and really looks me over, not even bothering to conceal it. I look quickly back to my work, and say something rather coolly about my getting on with it or I'd be here till midnight.

"He pulls away, says he'll be here way past midnight, and will be back in an hour on his rounds. Well, anyway, then he leaves and I hear his footsteps and the keys jingling, and in a moment I hear him stop. I look out, and there, down the corridor (I can see him from my office) he's standing in the shadows with his hand in front of him, touching himself very slowly, very deliberately, and looking over to see if I was looking. Which, of course, I was. But I turn back to my work immediately, and don't look back.

"In a minute I hear him continue on. Well, I start immediately pulling my things together to get out of there as quickly as I can. Then I start telling myself I've got to stay and finish the report I'm working on because it has to be ready first thing in the morning, and that I'm just imagining things, and there's no reason to be afraid.

"So I settle back down, go back to work, and keep an eye on my watch. And just before an hour passes, I get up to close my office door. I go back to work, and in a minute or two I hear his footsteps and keys jingling as he comes down the hall. I hear him stop outside my door. Then I hear some rustling sounds, another sound like keys being dropped on a desk, and another of coins spilling out on the floor. Then silence. Then a little soft movement, and a light knock on my door.

"'Sorry to bother you,' says he. Then I get very nervous.

"'I'm very busy,' I say.

"'I brought you something,' says he.

"'Oh, thanks,' say I. 'Would you just leave it out there. I'll pick it up on my way out.'

"'Well, I can't leave it,' he says. And the door opens

suddenly, and he's standing there absolutely naked. And ready for action, *quite* obviously.

"'I knew you'd still be here waiting,' he says. And while I'm looking absolutely horrified, he flicks out the light switch and kicks the door shut behind him.

"'You get the hell out of here,' I scream.

"'Calm down,' says he. 'There's no one around to hear you.'

"He grabs hold of me. Not brutally, or anything. But very forcefully.

"'Just relax,' he says. 'We're just going to have some fun.' Well, of course, we do. After a bit of struggle, naturally. On my desk. In my chair. On the floor. And I'm in seventh heaven. Until I get bored with the whole thing. Or disgusted with myself. Then I just come to, and that's that."

"Do you ever continue the daydream past this point?" I asked.

"I never think too much about what happens after we...after we've made it," she replied. "I mean, I don't think I've ever gotten into angry scenes, or calling the police, or I'll-be-working-again-tomorrow-night-will-you-be-here? or anything. I just have a little fun going through a few clinches, then I cancel out. And there you have it. Pat's big rape fantasy!"

Before Pat related her fantasy, we had discussed the fact that studies have shown that a common subject of women's sexual fantasies is rape. The most common rape fantasy involves being forced to submit to sex, and eventually enjoying it. Further, the most common psychological interpretation of these fantasies is that they do not signify that the subject in fact wishes to be raped, but, rather, wishes to indulge in the thought of sexual relations without guilt: "I couldn't help it. He made me do it."

"Oh, boy, that's me," Pat quipped. "If you hadn't told me that, I don't think I could tell you my favorite daydream. It's kind of mild as rape stories go, but I think it fits what you're talking about."

After she related her fantasy, Pat said, "I had always felt

surprised at myself about the rape part, because, believe me, the thought absolutely terrifies me. Now it makes a little more sense."

The wish to enjoy sexual relations with an attractive new partner could produce guilt. Fear of rape produces anxiety. Some psychological theories hold that rape fantasies offer a kind of two-in-one benefit in that they offer the imagined pleasures of sex without guilt and a calming vision of assault without pain. All of this occurs, of course, through the suppression of the true facts and circumstances of rape, and the true character of the rapist. But reality is not the game here—rather our attempts to cope with some of our fears, anxieties, and guilts about sex.

"I think the fantasy began," Pat continues, "when I was working late at the office, and was bored and unhappy at having to spend an evening working instead of playing. I felt extremely, almost ... ominously alone. I felt a little fearful and vulnerable. And, I think, *excited*, that anything could happen here and nobody would know. The opportunity for a fantasized incident with a watchman or guard, of course, soon presented itself. But most of these types I've ever encountered never turned me on. Simple enough, I guess, to invent a situation where I could conveniently slip someone attractive into the role.

"But I always enjoyed this fantasy. It seemed like the perfect place. I could put different people into the watchman's role and work up a little situation with each one, but it was always pretty much the same play, especially the parts about him touching himself in a very suggestive way, and undressing outside my door while I listened, and then suddenly appearing naked in front of me, which really excites me. . . . And, of course, I always do my best to resist.

"But listen, I'll tell you, I'm sure that if anyone pulled any of that on me in real life, I would just faint dead away. Well, maybe not that, but, wow, thanks, but no thanks."

Rape fantasies have many implications, as well as interpretations. Certainly they can be used to heighten one's sense of desirability. "Who wouldn't want to try to take me?" And they offer an opportunity to manipulate the man to act for the woman's pleasure—a reality not always common—by permitting the woman to consciously control his seemingly uncontrollable desire.

As guilt about sex can inspire a woman's rape fantasy, so fear of sex, fear of losing her power to the power-oriented male can inspire *raping* fantasies. Daydreams that depict men held powerless, kept in a harem, for instance, and called forth to perform at command can immobilize the fear of sex, the fear of losing identity and dignity in a sexual encounter. Each fantasy can have many different meanings, as many meanings as there are different kinds of fantasy themes. But each in its way helps us to cope with the emotions that sex excites.

A daydream of initiating a young male into the tender joys of sex neatly mixes good works with a bit of fun. Maneuvering a confirmed homosexual to the mat ambitiously combines good works, fun, and a deluxe ego trip. (Where everyone else has failed, I succeed.) Bedding down with one of the bigshots at work offers a grab bag of potential payoffs, not the least of which is upward mobility.

Studies have indicated that it is characteristic of women to fill their sexual fantasies, as Pat did, with plot and dialogue. Although at this time men's sexual fantasies have been studied much less fully than women's, it has been observed that their sexual fantasies are more purely visual, more concentratedly physical, as Jack's is.

Jack

"You want a daydream? I've got one for you. It's short and sweet, and it's been around with me a long time. And it still turns me on. I'm out in the country. There are a lot of willow trees. And beneath one of them this girl is lying naked in the snow, beautiful, with pale flesh, and red hair all spread out around her. She's waiting for me, and suddenly there I am, and we go right to it. I don't really think about the snow, or being uncomfortable or too cold or anything. I just think about how beautiful the image is: the red hair, the green willow trees, the white snow. And how warm and willing . . . and welcoming she is. It's really that simple. Nothing happens except that we make love. Oh, do we make love! And the thought of it makes me feel good."

What a glorious vision. Jack is at heart a Botticelli, serving up his delectable Venus on shaved ice instead of on the half shell. There she lies, a true goddess of love, promising a moment of glory in the driven snow. No battle of wits. No performance anxieties. No price tags. Just going to it, with the perfect partner in the perfect setting. A bit chilly, perhaps, and pristine. If it were the province of this book to interpret symbolism, Jack might provide a field day. His fantasy simplifies, glorifies, perhaps even purifies the sexual encounter. But it comes right to the point, and makes its erotic point perfectly.

Pat's fantasy is filmlike in its content, complete with sets and lighting, a sound track, and plenty of meaningful dialogue and plot for the heel and the heroine. Whether or not either fantasy needs to be classified here as typically male or typically female, it is interesting that Pat has gone to extraordinary lengths to permit herself the enjoyment of sex, whereas Jack cuts right to the perfect moment of consummation. Each effectively served its purpose as home entertainment and sexual stimulation, the one more titillating, suspenseful, and complicated in its payoffs, the other more uncomplicated, more forthrightly reveling in an expected pleasure.

Undoubtedly the structures of Jack's and Pat's fantasies have important relevance to their sex lives, their attitudes toward sex, and their present sex partners. Pat, who is in her early thirties, did indicate that a little more mystery and excitement, a little less of the automatic, taken-for-granted attitude might make her real love-life more complete.

And Jack, in his early forties, mentioned that his sex life

was not always anxiety-free and without emotional price tags. Surely their fantasies offered them interesting, stimulating compensations. And no doubt their fantasies tell us something about male and female social and sexual conditioning, and the role of power in sex. Jack seeks the compliant beauty. Pat summons the attractive beast.

Through the make-believe of daydreaming and fantasy we make sex what we will, performing as we choose and with whom we choose. The sight of someone attractive on the street or on the screen can get us started. Meeting a new person who looks just right to us can tempt us even more to a bit of lusty cerebration, as it did Wendy.

Wendy

"I think this is a sex fantasy, although I doubt whether it would ever get an X rating. Maybe an R. A few months ago, I took a driver training course so that I could finally get my license. And, as luck would have it, my instructor was very attractive, and it became really tough for me to concentrate on what I was doing.

"It made me nervous enough just trying to maneuver the car around without running into something. But I think most of my concentration was going toward wondering how he saw me. I remember thinking, would he like me more if I seemed really cool and unruffled, or would he pay more attention, be more sympathetic, if I seemed all sweet and flustered?

"Well we went along for a few lessons, and then I really became quite attracted to him. And daydreamed quite a bit about him. He had a mustache. I had never kissed anybody with a mustache, so I wondered what that would be like. And I began wondering what he might look like with his shirt off, and what it would feel like if he kissed me and I could feel his mustache and have my arms around him touching just skin.

"It didn't seem to perk up his interest in me whether I

played strong or helpless. I mean, he was very friendly and had an easy, comfortable manner about him, but there was no letdown in his professional attitude.

"But I still thought about him, and went still further with the necking daydreams and got so far as to imagine what it would be like if we were both undressed from the waist up, close, with our arms around each other. Then I wondered what his mustache would feel like against my breasts. Oh boy!

"In the fantasy all this went on when we would be driving along some quiet street in the evening, and he would suggest we practice parking—how clever of him—and things would just start happening. I thought about the possibility of things going further, but nothing really happened more than what I already told you. I didn't take it any further than the bare-breasted part.

"When I finally got the message that *nothing* was going to get started between us in real life, the daydreams stopped cold. I was probably a little pouty in my attitude toward him, maybe a little cold. In real life, I mean.

"I remember all along that I would fantasize how I might act to attract him. And I would use some of the fantasy material when I was with him. Not necessarily anything I would say, more to do with a look, or a smile. No. I'll take that back. I did manage to ask him whether or not he was married. Which is probably poison, no matter how nonchalantly I did it. Well, anyway, nothing in my bag of tricks seemed to work.

"Please don't get the idea I was blatantly trying to put the make on him or anything. All of this big talk was pretty much of a squeak when I was with him. I was just trying a few little things to attract him. At least I thought I was being subtle. Maybe he saw it all too clearly and was just tired of women coming on to him. He was very attractive, and I'm sure I wasn't the first to be attracted."

We talked about the gradual striptease effect of her daydream, and the growing eroticism that she had cut off suddenly. "That is pretty funny," she continued. "I guess even in my fantasies I go only so far. Heaven knows where it would have gone if he had shown any real interest. Linda Lovelace, sit down."

I asked Wendy if in real life, when she first met someone who was attractive to her, she considered behaving in a certain way to attract that person, as she had when she first met her driving instructor.

"Probably," she replied. "I've never been terribly sure of myself in the early part of any relationship. I'm not famous for casting spells. I do all right, but I must say the mind starts working on what to say or do that will get something going. And when it does, I probably look like a cat ready to pounce. I hope I don't. But I just don't have this carefully cultivated persona that some people seem able to project: 'This is me. I'm wonderful. Love me or leave me.' But I am usually able to relax enough to let things happen naturally if they're going to. I don't think it's a hang-up."

Our self-image is vitally important to us. Nowhere does its importance come home to us more than in our contacts with others, particularly those whose company we would like to keep. It isn't easy to relax, be ourselves, *and* be wonderful all at the same time. Sometimes we haven't the confidence and the patience to just "relax and let things happen," as Wendy put it. And sometimes, like football players before a game, or an actor before a performance, we like to psych ourselves up before plunging into battle.

Vera

"I am the siren. That's the image I get behind when I'm going out to a party. The clothes, the makeup, the mental attitude are all seductress. Understated, of course, but all there.

"While I'm getting ready to go out, I have visions of the effect I'll have when I arrive, and am introduced around. And there I am just intriguing the hell out of everyone: men walking away from women to come over to pay court, women turning green.

"I think the fantasies work for me in a couple of ways. In the first place they make getting ready a lot of fun, help me get over all the boring parts of preparation. And, of course, the mirror is there to watch the transformation from working girl to belle of the ball. That's fun.

"And the goal of making heads turn helps me feel special, more assured, more assured of having a good time. Much of the whole thing is focused on making a good entrance, like a ballerina making her first appearance."

I asked Vera how the seduction part goes in her daydreams.

"It doesn't," she replied with a laugh. "Although I usually have some sexy ideas about vamping someone and being carried off into the night by some likely suitor or other, all those thoughts usually fly right out of my head thirty seconds after I've made my entrance.

"I'm aware that people do look at me approvingly. But I usually get involved in the chatter and fun of it all right away and forget the whole siren thing. I am aware that I look good. But I don't slink around trying to seduce anyone. Women do not turn green with envy as far as I can see. Sometimes someone does sweep me off into the night. But not because of any Delilah act on my part.

"I think it's all part of getting myself up for having a good time, of getting high and going in expecting to have a good time, expecting fun things to happen. They usually do."

Vera is young, attractive, vivacious, fun to talk to. It would be difficult to think of her not having a good time at any party—or being successful as a seductress if she chose to be one, for that matter. If life is a ball, she is going as a vamp, which, when you think of what is probably in the back of the minds of most of the guests, isn't such a bad idea. Why she switches her act so abruptly to Miss Congeniality may reflect her own uncertainty as a sexpot in reality, or, more likely, her boredom with the too narrow dimensions of that role.

Whatever, she is determined to have a good time, knows how to get up a good flight plan in her head, and takes off for a predictably enjoyable evening. She gets over the boredom of getting ready, and the anxiety of getting into the swim, by imagining herself as the one we've all been waiting for.

What have we been waiting for? Tom is out looking for two girls "spreading the good news." Pat is waiting for the night watchman. Jack has a steady date with a snow angel. Wendy is waiting for someone to respond, preferably with a mustache. Vera, someone to "sweep me off into the night." Everyone makes their sex fantasies work for them in different ways, for different reasons. To escape boredom. To find a thrill. To try out a new lover. To search for a perfect love. To prepare for the moment the real thing might come along.

They sneak up on us whether we're ready for them or not. We can be in the middle of a task, in a moment of peace, and suddenly the show is on. Something may remind us of something, and off we go. Sometimes we call on them deliberately. We summon fantasies when we masturbate. We use them to warm us up for intercourse. Which can be a blessing and a curse.

Fantasies have remarkable turn-on power, but possess a strong turn-off capacity as well, for the fantasy we use during sex may trigger one of those three furies—guilt, anxiety, and fear—any one of which can put us under a cold shower in seconds.

If the person we're thinking of and the person we're having sex with are not one and the same, we may begin to have guilt feelings, which might inhibit our enjoyment. Men who fear too early a climax may summon nonsexual images, even running the alphabet backward, to keep things going, then suddenly find themselves going nowhere somewhere between M and L. If we're deter-mined to make a wild night of it, but remember our failure the last wild night out, we may not even get started.

Sex researchers Masters and Johnson have identified fears of inadequacy as a major deterrent to effective sexual functioning. Some of those fears can be triggered when our feelings about our real selves, our real partners, what we really do together do not measure up to our fantasies about sex and our sexual selves. And we can suffer from "fantasy gap."

If you have it, and you can't talk yourself out of it, think of talking it over fully and frankly with your partner. Track down the recommended books on the subject. If talking and reading don't help, ask your doctor to recommend a counselor or therapist. Do what you can to free yourself of the anxieties that keep you from the joy you may seek.

Of course, there are many who can and do enjoy fantasies during sex to enhance and sustain their enjoyment and performance. Creatures of hearty appetite, they are blissfully immune to Cupid's dirty tricks, untouched by fantasy gap, undeterred by the way-out nature of some of their sexual daydreams.

Our daydreams can sometimes cater to the bizarre as our minds attempt to cope with our sexual curiosities and anxieties, sometimes reworking those that first occurred when we were children. The more punishment and inhibition we experienced about sex when we were children, the more bizarre those daydreams might have become.

Yet in the long run, unless we are in the throes of sexual dysfunction, there seems to be little need for alarm about kinky fantasies. Psychiatrist Dr. Willard Gaylin, quoted by Martha Weinman Lear in the March 1973 issue of *McCall's*, says:

> Our fantasies are built-in escape valves, and we must never
> feel guilty about them. Masochism and sadism,
> exhibitionism, voyeurism, homosexuality, group sex—
> anything you can think of—they're all ways of handling our
> anxiety. Way out? Of course. They're supposed to go way
> out. That's what fantasies are for.

Our fantasies don't always wander the streets seeking out the new and the different. We can use them to enhance our ongoing relationships, too. Those we love figure prominently in our daydreams, as they do in our real lives.

Fran

"I'm not sure this is a fantasy, but it involves many...images that all add up to what I would call daydreaming. I've always had a wonderful relationship with Bill—emotionally, physically, everything. We've argued a lot over the years [Fran is in her fifties and has been married over thirty years] but we've always made up and gone on and become more involved with each other than ever.

"The only one in my sexual fantasies is Bill. And there's no real story to them, just fleeting images of being in bed with him, being close. They're terribly reassuring, very much...reminding me I'm a very fortunate person. But for years I've been aware that if I'm angry with him, or disappointed in him for some reason or other, it...cancels out my sexual feelings. If he would attempt to initiate sex, I would have fantasies of resistance, of being unable to enjoy, or even go through with sex while I had these angry feelings. I would see him saying or doing the things that had hurt, and I would dwell on them to keep myself cool, unmovable, unresponsive.

"But in the long run, that kind of behavior made me so miserable, and I felt childish, petulant because of it. And I began to adopt a *modus operandi* that has worked like a charm. I simply never allow negative feelings to build up without talking about them almost immediately to Bill. I mention my feelings to him, he responds, we talk it over, we work it out, and we go to bed happy, or at least peaceful.

"For a long time now there have been no negative, no judgmental fantasies when time for sex comes around. Only anticipation, feelings of pleasure and...love."

I asked Fran if, when she had angry feelings, she withdrew from sex because of her lessened sexual feelings, or to punish her husband for his transgressions. "Probably both," she replied, "but I think it was more the first one, the lessened sexual feelings. Sex is certainly a giving of yourself, and I think it's very difficult to give when you don't believe. That's why I think it finally dawned on me that you had better keep the believing part, the understanding and trust, the no-holding-grudges part strong and clear, and do it, literally, on a day to day basis. It works for me."

Fran objected to the negative fantasies that interfered with her life, and took steps to weed them out. Positive ones, of course, are to be cherished and nurtured. Paul's fantasies give him a sense of the past that sustains, renews, and regenerates his present affections.

Paul

Paul is in his early sixties and has been married to Dorothy almost forty years.

"I have had fantasies of all kinds in my life, particularly when I was younger. And of course I had fantasies about sex. All kinds. The one that's been most important to me, in the last ten or fifteen years particularly, is one I use just before and during sex. It arouses me, gets me going in the most wonderful way. And keeps me going. I think of Dorothy and myself making love when we were barely out of our teens.

"I think of how she looked and how I looked, and some special nights that I still remember after many years. It isn't always from our twenties. Sometimes it's later, much later. And it isn't specifically a memory in the sense of trying to recall specific details.

"It is more a sense memory of many, many happy moments over the years, all jumbled up in this great kaleidoscope of youthful flesh and middle-aged passion and, as I like to call it, 'late love,' which is what I'm beginning now, I guess.

"It's every bit as good now as it ever was. The only difference that I can see is that I'm not as easily aroused as when I was twenty. So the fantasy comes in handy to . . . crank things up. It began, by the way, when I began to feel a bit guilty about using images of someone else to give me a little extra lift when I was making love to Dorothy. One night many years ago I just began thinking about us when we were kids, and it worked like a charm. It has really helped keep sex very special, something I can feel good about, like forty years is not such a long time after all."

A good image of ourselves and our partners, and images that reinforce the happiness of being together would seem to be priceless assets in an ongoing love affair. Love isn't all physical. As Wordsworth expressed it in his poem, "Strange Fits of Passion":

> What fond and wayward thoughts will slide
> Into a lover's head!

The better to love you with, my dear.

IV. POWER

I'd love to gain complete control of you,
And handle even the heart and soul of you.
                                        Cole Porter,
                                        "All of You"

Some people want it all. Your heart. Your soul. Your body. Your paycheck. Your full attention. Your vote. Your wristwatch. Your job. Your applause. Whatever it is they have this terrible need for, they'll try to get, one way or the other. If you're ripe for the taking, they won't rest until you've been taken. Now you may comfort yourself that God loveth a cheerful giver. But have you noticed how well those cheerful takers do?

For one thing, they always seem to have such good addresses. Something with "Place," or at least "Park" in it. And they're turned out so well. In sheep's clothing, usually. And if their fine gazes cloud over every few seconds as you speak with them, do be alarmed. Their feverish brains are running scenarios of how they will get the upper hand. The better to wield the power they crave.

Now I'm not just talking about Macbeth and Richard III. Or Hitler and Napoleon. Or any of a number of today's high-stakes power players who spend their summers on Olympus and their winters in minimum security facilities. I'm talking about power lovers everywhere. It could be your mother, the headwaiter at your least favorite restaurant, the man who got your vote for assemblyman, your secretary, or the cop on your beat. Look in the mirror. It could be you. I looked into mine. I wasn't Snow White.

The truth is we all love power. To watch how some of us scramble for it so ruthlessly and others hold on to it so graciously is to enjoy some of the best parts of the human comedy. Most of us were born professionals at the power game. As babies we knew what we wanted and usually got it with a loud cry, an adorable gurgle, or a disgusting mess. As small children we could easily sway a roomful of foolish adults with a cunning smile or a simple trick. (Isn't she cute?) (Isn't he a terror?)

But then, bit by bit, those vicious adults took their toll. Mommy spanked. Daddy took away our allowance. Miss Pringle sent us to the principal's office. Professor Bliffle gave us a D. We learned to be nice, do what we were told, and abandon power to the more powerful. We learned, too, the primitive rituals of the pecking order.

Sometimes we learned not to abandon power, merely to concede it when necessary. And to wait our turn. Which is one of the things that makes living with others so interesting. You can't always tell who's waiting for what.

While we're waiting, we can have these terrific fantasies about what it's going to be like when we get our turn. Mistress of the manor. King of the hill. Caller of the shots. Whoopee!

Gary

"Ever since I was a teen-ager the biggest, shiniest truth that kept coming home to me was that power is money, money is power. If you could get the money to get what you wanted, you had the feeling of power. If I wanted something, and I couldn't get it, I felt caught. I felt like life just had to stop till I could figure out a way to get it.

"If I would see a bike or something that I really wanted,

I'd have fantasies about how cool I would be once I got it. *Top cat.* And I'd spend a lot of time hatching up a scheme to get it. My poor father was usually the first target, because the first thing that would occur to me, naturally, was to somehow get him to give me what I wanted.

"Well, I'd stay awake nights trying to work out some speech or other that would convince him my life depended on his getting me that bike, or whatever it was that I just had to have. The more I wanted it, the better the speech would be. Now you have to understand that my dad was terrific to me. I don't think he ever spoiled me, but he was generous. So he was approachable on most things. I was never afraid to ask.

"But as I got older he began with the speeches that things couldn't always be had for the asking, that money wasn't always available, that I needed to concentrate more on books and less on just messing around. And of course I didn't buy any of that. No way.

"I wasn't much of a student, and I wasn't a real jock. I think what started developing was that I got my buzz on *having* things, maybe things nobody else had, or a little bit better than they had. Of course, the car got to be the big thing. Four-wheeled charm, and all that. I remember actually giving my father a big speech about having to have a car so that I could be a leader.

"Well, that produced a big scene, and a big speech about values. But after a while we worked out a deal where we each would put up half. And I worked my butt off for one summer and one whole school year after work, and I finally got the old Chevy I wanted."

Gary and I talked at length about his goals, about life in general, about his image of himself.

"It's important to me to have a nice home, cars, vacations, plenty of money, good things for my family. Getting them really wasn't—or isn't—all that hard. I think very early I just put two and two together, figured out I liked things, and liked having the image of being a go-getter, of being someone who lived well. I figured out that you had to work for it, and knew I'd have to work for it because there was nothing special about me that would cause it to just drop in my lap.

"Right now I fantasize a lot about the regional managership I'll be moving into in the fall. A vice-presidency goes with it, and I have a feeling it's about as far as I'm going. I've been with them almost twenty years [he is with a large steel company] and it's taken some doing to get this far, so I'm pleased as hell it's happening.

"I've had my eye on this job for five years. I've figured I could handle it for the last three or four. For about a year now I've known that the man who has the job is taking an early retirement and that I had the inside track. So I've been thinking about how I'll handle the job, and what it will do for my life. I can sit in his office talking with him and see my pictures on his desk, think through how I would handle the situation we're talking about if I were in charge. I can't wait to get in that chair.

"I think about the guys who are now my peers, and I dream up little scenes about how they'll react to me in the job and how I'll handle them. I think about who I might fire, who I might promote, and try to imagine how they'll react to me as the boss, the man who could say 'You stay,' or 'You go.'

"This morning I daydreamed all the way to the office about maybe moving. Marilyn and I have talked about it, but the real estate business is so crazy now. And I thought about getting a new car—something new for the new image."

In a recent study of male fantasies undertaken by psychologist Leonard Giambra at the Gerontology Research Center of the National Institute on Aging, and reported in *Psychology Today* (December 1974), it was observed that problem solving, not sex, was the predominant topic in most age groups, except the youngest, ages seventeen to twenty-three, where it was a tie. His studies further concluded that "daydreams about sex and achievement decline steadily with age."

Referring to psychologist Eric Klinger's theories that

"daydreams reflect current concerns, interests and problems of the individual," and that "they act as an alternate channel in effect, a mental backburner, in which information can be organized and reorganized creatively," Giambra concludes that "the fact that problem solving heads the list of daydream types supports this interpretation."

Although it was impossible to coax any specific fantasies in detail from Gary, it was clear that he used fantasy as a "mental backburner" to help him chart the course of his life. Many of his wants and needs, like those of many of us, were materialistic. ("That's no dirty word to me," he said.) It was simple enough to try out, in his mind, a new car, a new home, to check out the feel it gave him before he set out to get it. In the same way, to facilitate his getting more of the things he wanted, he could fantasize about getting to the next corporate level in his career—how he would react, what he would do, how he would qualify.

I asked Gary how he felt about the "boss" part of power, about being the man in control. "I like it, and it's always been important to me. But it's not the big thing with me that it is with some people. I like to think of myself as an executive, as a man with power, as a man who lives well and can hold up his head anywhere. Obviously the means to that end is my job. The better I do, the more I get.

"People boss me. I boss people. It's like a game. And I've always been pretty good at games. The company says its goals are such and such. They pay me to help reach those goals. I have no problems with that arrangement.

"But I don't really need to be boss. When I said a minute ago that I thought I wasn't going to go much further up the line, I meant it. There are people who really need to be top cat, whose big thing is power. From my experience those are the ones who usually fight it out or finagle their way toward the top perches. The ones who have to be on top. I'm just not that driven. Motivated, yes, but not driven. The motivation is having money, living well, not being commander-in-chief."

Gary used fantasy not only to conceive his goals, but also to maneuver his way toward them. He appraised himself realistically ("I could think clearly, and I was always organized. The best place for those qualifications is business.") He accepted that self-appraisal, and set about achieving the good life he wanted for himself and his family, lighting his way with fantasy. And with each step, he asserted himself and enhanced his feelings of having power.

The fear of losing power can be as potent as the desire and drive to achieve power, and can prompt fantasies and motivate behavior just as urgently, as Louise, my beautiful friend from chapter I, makes clear.

Louise

"As a child I had always been told I was pretty, and I remember it gave me pleasure and made me feel special. But I can't tell you the problems it brought when I reached adolescence. It seemed I continually had to cope with advances, quite early, even from members of my family. And I found it all very difficult to handle, particularly at first when my emotional responses made me feel guilty, made me feel as though I were a bad person.

"To make matters worse, I could tell my mother was beginning to feel competitive with me. She seemed to be, at least to my mind, less kind, less motherly to me as I grew toward adulthood. I felt less and less secure day by day, until the thought dawned on me that if I were not attractive perhaps the advances would stop, and my mother would . . . well, love me again. It was a dilemma, and a painful one. I enjoyed the power my looks seemed to give me, but I felt threatened, confused, unhappy at the responses it brought out in others. I just didn't know how to handle it.

"Before long I deliberately cultivated a sloppiness in my appearance, and drifted into a kind of cool withdrawal. And to some extent it worked. The seductive behavior of the men lessened, and my mother seemed to warm up considerably. But the withdrawal, of course, was damaging.

"I spent a great deal of time alone in my room with all kinds of fantasies, many of them normal, I suppose, for a young teen-age girl. But I look back on that period as the beginning of anxieties about myself and about others that still cling to me.

"I had fantasies of giving in to the advances that men, young and old, seemed to lavish on me. I had fantasies of being the perfect child no mother could fail to love. I saw myself as the model of responsive behavior, seeking and getting approval right and left. But I also fantasized mutilating myself in some way to rid myself of all the problems my looks seemed to pose. And I had fantasies of getting revenge on men—my mother, too—for all the embarrassment and guilt and uncertainty they made me feel.

"I had very fanciful daydreams about being a great beauty and breaking hearts, like the heroine in *Great Expectations*. Then I began fantasizing about other ways to overcome being pretty than just making myself unattractive. My family was musical, and I dreamed of becoming a pianist and being thought of as gifted, talented. That was really intoxicating.

"I bought scores of records—Tchaikovsky, Brahms, Schumann—and played them over and over pretending that it was me playing them. I planned what I would wear, what kind of gown, and so on. I played under different conductors, and I amazed each one with my virtuosity. And, of course, I always had a picture of who was in the audience at the time. Always my mother, and a selection of teachers and friends and enemies—well, not enemies, rather people I may have been hurt by, or felt anxious about.

"Of course there were wonderful scenes in the dressing room or backstage afterwards with everyone acknowledging the brilliant new me, not the beautiful bad Louise, but the serious and accomplished artist Louise.

"Well, all of these images literally enveloped me, and

that's when my musical endeavors began in earnest. [Louise today is a pianist of great accomplishment and a performing artist of growing prestige.] The pleasure and sense of accomplishment I got from experiencing my growth as a musician truly helped me through that difficult, sensitive period. And many of the acute anxieties and problems in my life just faded away.

"Until the next blow came, that is. And that was when my mother, at some point in my later teens, began getting on me about my grooming and appearance. I had maintained a very low profile and had cultivated an image of being serious and dedicated. Now her message was that it was time for me to start playing up my looks and getting the kind of man she thought I might expect to get. Her whole point seemed to be that I should begin working on my 'salability.'

"And suddenly I felt myself back in that deadly business of being the pretty one, actually this time of flaunting myself at people whose intentions I had learned not to trust, or at least to be wary of. I thought about my music and probably having to give it up to be the consort of some likely candidate or other. I felt terribly angry. I felt victimized. I saw myself losing the power that I had so eagerly cultivated—the music—that was giving me such a growing feeling of security.

"Well, this time the fantasies ran the gamut from flight to suicide to martyrdom to God knows what. It was one of the most miserable times of my life. But nothing that I tried out in my mind seemed to provide a logical answer. And the truth is, that as I matured I was as attracted to men as they seemed to be attracted to me."

Louise eventually did put aside her music and accepted what she came to feel were the unavoidable roles of marriage and motherhood. Her two marriages, each of some duration and some happiness, ended unhappily.

"Most of the problems that arose in my marriages and later life derived absolutely from those uncertain early years and the awful anxieties we've talked about. I think what has helped me most is just time, a little more maturity, and the almost relentless desire to find out who I am, to know my own power, not just to live in so responsive a way to other people.

"But my self-image is much improved from those early years and from the difficult periods in my marriages. I feel more comfortable with my looks—a little vanity probably here and there—but I accept them and am glad for them. Now they're very much a part of my identity, part of my sense of being me, and I try to protect them. For instance, even though my friends laugh, I stay out of the sun religiously to keep my skin from being damaged. [Louise has the kind of clear, pale glow that the ladies of Lola Montez's day literally died to get.] I've learned to live with people's responses to my looks, negative and positive, and to enjoy the positive parts.

"Most of all I enjoy having my music again. I love performing and the kind of restored sense of self it's giving me. It had hurt so to give it up. But I had never felt sure that I wasn't using it to divert people's attention away from my looks. And I couldn't be sure that it wasn't just a fantasy that I could be accepted at something other than face value. Now I'm comfortable with them both together, and it's a good feeling. I remember going out and buying a pair of glasses I didn't need, to wear for an audition for a master class, and wearing severe clothing, all in hope that I would be taken seriously as a musician. I don't do that anymore."

Alfred Adler, the Austrian psychiatrist who founded the school of individual psychology, theorized that each individual has a wish or need for power and self-assertion, that when these wants are thwarted by our environment, feelings of inferiority and a pattern of neurotic maladjustment can follow.

In our dreams and daydreams we can compensate for our feelings of inferiority, or sense of failure and humiliation, by conjuring up scenes of success and admiration. In real life, Adler suggested, individuals who suffer from personal disabilities may seek a pattern of overcompensation, may try to overcome their sense of deficiency by unusual achievement. From this theory have come the suggestions that Napoleon's drive for glory derived from the need to compensate for his short stature, that Byron's poetic achievements sprang from his desire to overcome the handicap of a clubfoot.

Much that is beautiful and ugly in the world has been created by those with an extraordinary need to discover and assert themselves, or to exert and make manifest their longing for power, however they came by that need. The histories of art and war, filled with accounts of those who sought and found impressive achievement, illustrate the broad range of the uses of power.

Michelangelo and Hitler were overachievers, perhaps overcompensators, whose inspiration and accomplishments were of such magnitude they define the limits of earthly power. The works of one are precious to us, lovingly housed and shown, perfect idealizations of our physical selves and our spiritual reach. The works of the other are perhaps even better known, clearly marked on grave sites around the world and in the eyes of those still living who viewed his works at close range.

Neither had happy lives, in the mundane sense of the word. But who among us will know the ecstatic sense of power Michelangelo must have felt when he completed his work in the Sistine Chapel. Or the dizzying sense of self Hitler must have felt in the midst of a torchlight rally, with thousands of impassioned voices hailing his name, worshiping his presence.

Most of us neither possess the inspiration nor suffer the need to overachieve. To captivate hearts and minds, to command pledges of allegiance en masse may not be beyond our imaginations, but such goals are beyond our real aspirations and our reach.

In our social and political organizations we have made it a practice to cede power to those with the drive and capacity to take it, and, hopefully, the ability to handle it. We elect them, promote them, support them. We allow them to color our world, change our lives. When they overstep themselves, show ineptitude, or merely bore us, we conspire to bring them down, and search among other power players for a new, more promising leader, figure-head, symbol, seer.

And while they strut and fret in life's larger arenas, we stay at home and play our power games on a more microcosmic scale. We boss, and are bossed. We concede, and seek concessions. We grab, and get slapped. We argue and compromise. And we do it around the clock. Getting our way is very time-consuming.

One of the ways we spend our time is watching how the successful power players do it, and we use them as role models.

Dora

Dora is a popular New York hostess—bright, attractive, high-spirited, kind, real, no stranger to the power game.

"I have had fantasies of being Anne Summers [an extraordinarily wealthy woman whom Dora admires]. Or being *like* her, I think is putting it more accurately. The power that her wealth gives her is, to me, staggering to think about. It isn't just the good life she has. I have that, or enough of it at least. I mean there are entire enterprises, causes, movements that depend on her goodwill and leadership.

"She can literally make things happen, is on top of it all. What a great feeling that must be—to be constantly in motion, no blocks, no waiting for a favorable wind, just go. Now. What you want to happen, happens. What you don't want to happen, doesn't. I'm sure it's not as simple as all that, but it's unreal to think what she can do.

"I've had glimpses of her life-style. I've seen how she holds forth. When things are not going too well for me on one of my little escapades, I sometimes think of Anne and how she would cope with my problem, how she could cope with it. I think what intrigues me most is her attitude—calm, sure, let's-talk-it-over, do-it, and do-it-right. She's never overbearing. She has too much style for that. What she has is that rare kind of authority with grace. And it's *that* that I want to emulate."

I asked Dora if there were specific scenes, or any recurring images of Anne Summers that she called to mind.

"I don't think so," she replied. "Most of my thoughts about her are fleeting ones. When we were talking before, about how we use daydreams in problem solving, that's what made me think of Anne. And just now, when I said I think about her when I have a problem, it seems obvious I use her as a kind of role model. 'Here's how she would handle it in her position. Perhaps that's the best solution for me.'

"I've used models all my life to shape my way of doing things, of thinking about things. Teachers, friends I admire, writers, people I read about. And power is such a big number. I mean some people are so outrageous when they get it. And it's something we all react to so violently when it's abused. It's wonderful to have someone like Anne to look to. She does it all so well."

There are many role models available to us in life, and the models we choose, who become part of our fantasy life, say much about the way we think, the way we plan, the paths we choose. Sally chose the royal road. Brush up your bows and curtsies. Here comes the Queen.

Sally

"I've had this thing about Queen Elizabeth [II] ever since I was quite young and watched her marriage and her coronation on television. I did a lot of pretending in those days, and there was no doubt about it, I was the Queen. I was utterly fascinated by her, all the pomp and pageantry that were part of her life, the crowns and coaches, the royal cast of characters—I just inhaled it all. I really began taking on this image of myself as a very special person. And I think it played a very important part in my personality development."

Sally doesn't come on as though she were reviewing the troops, or being amused from her viewpoint in the royal box, nor has she led an overprotected existence. She is very real, extraordinarily buoyant, conversant, intelligent, with perhaps too much of a free spirit to make an ideal figurehead. But her poise and charm and good looks could make a queen envious. And popular.

"I have used that image of myself as a queen many times to my advantage in the past. And I still use it. For instance, I know this isn't consistent with my image, but I do cry a lot. More, I think, from tender feelings than anything else. A Coca-Cola ad could do it. The kids are so bored with it at this point, when they see it coming, they say, 'Oh, Mother, not again.' But if I am in a situation where I feel I'm about to disgrace myself, I think of myself as the Queen, who doesn't do such things, and I don't. I run an image of myself as having all eyes on me, everyone expecting me to behave perfectly. *Voilà*. No tears.

"It really worked for me some years ago when I was working for the Peace Corps in the Pacific. To begin with I was automatically a celebrity: the fair-skinned goddess from America, and all that. And I, of course, played it to the hilt. The queen of the jungle. Something unfortunate happened that put me in the limelight even more. My friend and co-worker was killed in a plane crash in the jungles of one of the nearby islands. We held a funeral service for her in our community before her body was shipped back to the States. It had shocked all of us on the island, and the service was quite a public occasion. Some of the natives were avid photographers. They photographed everything: births, deaths, any excuse to get the flashbulbs going.

"Well, it was the role of my career. All eyes were on me. And given my predisposition to tears, I was terrified of making a spectacle of myself. Until I remembered Elizabeth, and that quiet, smiling, regal bearing. And it was instant transferral. I became Queen Sarah at a state occasion. I had fantasies of how I would handle myself, how it would all go. And I followed them right down the line.

"Photographers were leaping out from behind palm trees every three seconds, and I played it to the hilt. Queen Sarah was a hit. It was a long time and a million miles away from all those royal tea parties with my dolls. But there it was in all its glory: the continuing adventures of the Queen."

I asked Sally if, in her identification with Elizabeth, there were feelings of being powerful, if the fantasies and her acting out of them prompted in her any assertions of power in her behavior.

"None I can think of," was her reply. "Only in my feelings of power over myself, of controlling my behavior in a way to appear poised, unruffled...ceremonious. I think, after all, that was the whole fascination with Elizabeth to begin with as a child. All the pomp and circumstance, the great ceremonial aspect of everything she did, or everything that I saw that she did, was the appeal. It certainly made me feel important, but I wouldn't say powerful, at least not in the off-with-their-heads aspect of power. Anyway, as far as real power goes, she is a relatively passive figure. As I just said of myself, *important, but not powerful.*"

To those of us with active imaginations, how we appear to ourselves and how we appear to others can be critical, particularly when we are thrust into new and trying situations. Maintaining our poise, our "cool," seems essential, and a role model can be powerful assistance.

While I was speaking with Sally, her older brother Alex joined the conversation, and he gave gently humorous confirmation of Sally's early identification with royalty. Some indication was given that the Queen's subjects, Alex namely, were not always willing ones. ("We fought a lot," Sally admitted.)

"My greatest fantasy, or pretense, or whatever you want to call it, was to carefully make sure that everything I did appeared to be done effortlessly," Alex admitted.

"He was so perfect," Sally laughed. "He made me ill. No wonder I became Queen. It was the only way I could get an edge."

Ah, when fantasies collide. Getting the psychological advantage over others is a power game we have all played at one time or another. Who and what we seem to be has always been a heavy part of the game. We use fantasies to control ourselves, and we fight to gain control of the fantasies of others. The cleverest among us know that appearances are everything. The most gullible among us believe that what appears to be, *is*.

If you can muster the appearance of power, you can hold sway over imaginations. Thrones, processions, robes, crowns, palaces, fast cars, limousines, motorcades, aides, guards, armies, lies, rhetoric, manifestos, a ruthless manner, a charming manner, "dedication," noble causes, "the truth," a public relations department, ceremonies, a full portfolio—latch on to any three of these big numbers from the arsenal of power and you're on your way. You will have followers.

But holding sway over imaginations and having followers is a little too hyperthyroidal for most of us. A modest satisfaction with ourselves and the lives we lead is usually enough. And if we borrow a few tricks of the trade from the giants every now and then to get our way, who's to know?

Sometimes we can release some of the frustrations, some of that creeping sense of powerlessness by assuming, in our fantasies, a bit of supreme power. Which, of course, unleashes some of our more ruthless and primitive instincts.

Frank

"When I was a kid I had this recurring fantasy of getting rid of other kids in my class who for some reason or other were bothering me. It was like a game I played with myself when

I was bored, which was often, as I remember. I would just sit there and mentally check off the offenders and imagine them being carried off.

"I remember dispatching them in different ways, depending on what I may have read in some comic book the night before, or on TV or whatever. I remember once I sent them off with those funny monkey-looking creatures that worked for the Wicked Witch of the West in *The Wizard of Oz*. And another time I remember seeing a movie in which someone sitting at a desk had the power of sending people to heaven or hell. When they sent them to hell they pressed a little button on the desk, and the floor opened under the sendee and they fell down into flames and smoke. That became a favorite way to get rid of those I didn't want around.

"I don't remember if I had any pet hates. It probably started with someone who beaned me with a book or kicked me or something. But I do remember it became a game, because I think sooner or later I got around to everybody. On some days if I felt dumb, I sent all the smart ones away. If I felt smart I pushed the button on all the dumb ones. If I felt tough, the weaklings got it. But there I was, this little Hitler in the making, just playing God with everybody in sight.

"I'll tell you something funny. I still play the game. A couple of friends and I one crazy night hatched the scheme of setting up a charter flight for a very special group of people, all of them with reserved seats. The plane would take off, but never land.

"We reserved seats for a large number of people— usually always public figures, people in show business or sports or politics—whom we hated or couldn't stand. Sometimes still, in conversation or whatever, we'll refer to some doomed celebrity with a 'He's getting on that plane.' If there's some doubt, or some hope for him, or her, we put them on standby."

Our daydreams and fantasies offer us unlimited doses of power with which to amuse ourselves, and relieve some of the frustrations with people and circumstances in our lives. It's intoxicating to play God in our imagination, and just sweep away those who oppose or annoy us. They have such an irritating way of hanging around in real life.

As children, many of us were suddenly and frighteningly introduced to concepts of heaven and hell and what might happen to bad little boys and girls if they didn't straighten up and fly right. Small wonder that our dreams and fantasies didn't feature our being unmercifully speared by the devil or mauled by the Big Bad Wolf. Or, to maintain our sanity, that we didn't imagine ourselves as the all-powerful one who meted out all that punishment and sent everybody else to their just deserts. Better to be the sender than the sendee.

Our fantasy world need have no moral code. We commit no real crimes. We needn't fear real punishment. We need feel no guilt for any real transgression. We can release our hostilities in a no-man's-land, look at them, laugh at them, and get back to the serious business of trying to be decent to one another, a bit lighter of heart than before. At least until the next person crosses us.

Karen

"I'm developing a hate for bicyclists who don't observe traffic rules. They've become such a hazard in the city, running through red lights, jumping up onto sidewalks, zigzagging in and out of traffic. I've seen them knock people down and hurt them. They have scared the hell out of me more times than I can count, and I'm really getting fed up with them all.

"I've begun yelling at them when they try to pull a fast one. But that's not always the smartest thing to do in this town. Now when one of them gets my blood up, I concoct some pretty brutal fantasies, usually matching them up with the bumper of a Mack truck. Splat! One less offender.

"I'm sure my own frustration level has something to do with it. Some days it doesn't take much to get me started.

But navigating New York streets seems to get worse every year. I react the same way with taxi drivers, the ones who are always running the lights, and roaring through crowded crosswalks, making life miserable for pedestrians. They're going to be extinct in a few years anyway at the prices they're charging, but I've hurried more than a few along with fantasies of their meeting up with this nice big light pole."

New York is a city of power. Empires rise and fall daily in its skyscraping board rooms. But nowhere are games of power played more furiously and with greater flair than down below in the streets. Block by block, car drivers, cab drivers, bus drivers, truck drivers, horse and carriage drivers, motorcylists, bicyclists, tricyclists, skate boarders, roller skaters, baby carriage pushers, joggers, marchers, walkers, stragglers, and tipplers bluff and bull their way along as though there were no tomorrow. To watch who gets through an intersection at rush hour, and how they do it, is to learn what looking out for number one is all about.

Pedestrians are, of course, the most vulnerable. They are also, oddly enough, the most provocative. If they're light on their feet and fully covered, the sky's the limit. A commanding air is helpful, too.

Once, some years ago, as I gazed from my second-floor office window—daydreaming, probably—I looked across the street and watched a taxi stop in the middle of the block. An elegantly dressed woman emerged. Since Madison Avenue traffic went both ways in those days, it was necessary for her to wait for a lull in traffic in both directions before she could cross the street.

I guessed that her destination was my building, whose entrance was right under my window. I gave her about half an hour to make the crossing. But in about twenty seconds she tired of the game, stepped out into traffic, held up her arm majestically as though she were Moses parting the Red Sea, stopped traffic dead, and made it across to the center line with a light skip.

She then lifted her arm to stop traffic coming in the

other direction, beginning to make a game of it and smiling
radiantly. It was then I recognized her as Loretta Young.
Traffic, of course, stopped dead once again. And Miss
Young, looking pleased with herself, as well she might
have been, danced lightly to the curb, as though she had
just opened that door and waltzed onto her set, and
disappeared through the entrance beneath me. That, I
thought, was *power*.

And that, I thought, would be the way I would get mine
if I ever tried it. People well rehearsed and long practiced in
the ways of power and assertive behavior dare to do much
that those of us who are less assertive, or less practiced,
might never try.

How do they do it? Well, they practice. They first
determine how much and what kind of power they want
and need. They determine that in their heads, envisioning
themselves doing what they deem to be important and
self-propelling, and being *successful* at it. They then try it. If
they fail, they try again. If they fail a little less, they try
again. If they begin to succeed, they keep at it. When they
succeed, they keep on doing it.

When they keep on doing it, the best develop a certain
style, that all-important quality that Dora spoke of as
"authority with grace." At this point, the world is usually
their oyster, an oyster that tastes quite like their fantasy
said it would. Charming, determined, and careful, they do
not appear to be overly aggressive. But they will not suffer
much exploitation. They seem to know who they are, what
they want, and how to get it. And if what they want is on
the other side of Madison Avenue, be prepared to stop and
let them pass.

Nearly everything we do involves some kind of assertion
of power, or adjustment or reaction to the power needs of
others. Life is a game of power. Between getting and giving
we seek a dignified balance. When the scales tip against us,
we react. We want to "get as good as we give."

The getting and the giving start in the head, in the
picture we have of ourselves, the success story we see for
ourselves. If we see ourselves consistently taking, or giving

away, too much power, we should look to the motivation, the possible neurosis that could be throwing us off balance, throwing us into conflict with others and within ourselves.

And, of course, we must be as good at daring and doing as we are at dreaming. If we don't put our hearts and backs into what we have imagined for ourselves, we will never pass "Go," much less monopolize any of the good things life has to offer.

The ones who pull it off best know how to dream and dare and do. We have to watch out for the ones who would dare, to requote Cole Porter's lyric, "to take complete control" of us. Those who would "handle the heart and soul" of us approach at their own risk.

Lee is a cabaret singer and a person who seems to embody most of life's best gifts. When I first spoke with her I had hoped to find some kind of fantasy involving glory, but what she spoke of involved power, the capacity to reach out and touch, perhaps even handle, another's heart and soul.

Lee

"When I was doing light operatic singing, at the very beginning of my career, I do remember fantasies of glorious entrances and perfect high notes and applause and being swamped with offers. But that kind of fantasy disappeared early for me. What remains is this overriding image of myself as someone who has something special to give, and it's my *mission* to vindicate that feeling, to share what I have, to enjoy feeling special while I try to make others feel special.

"Now that I'm doing club work, I do have one fantasy that recurs. I think of myself singing, concentrating, communicating with just one person, or one couple. The goal, I think, is to touch them, to make them feel what I feel, what the composer felt, what the lyricist felt. Everything I do, when I perform, flows out of that image.

And I keep that image very close when I'm preparing and planning new material, or working a new room. I think I've spent more time imagining myself singing than I've spent singing."

In the intimate club atmosphere in which Lee thrives, the one-on-one approach is essential. And when she sings, we are literally in her power, allowing her to touch our hearts. Which she does with grace. Her fantasy touches on an important facet of power. We do, and must, surrender it to others from time to time, to hear them out, allow them sway, enjoy the pleasures of compromise, explore the possibilities of communion.

As with love and fair play, power is a matter of give and take. If, as Lord Acton suspected, "power tends to corrupt, and absolute power corrupts absolutely," it would become us to share and give away power as readily as we take and hold it. No one lives forever. We own nothing. No one. Only the right to seek our own dignity, and the obligation to allow others theirs.

The problem with most dreams of power is that they inevitably start like this lyric from Alfred Bunn's libretto for the opera, *The Bohemian Girl*:

> I dreamt that I dwelt in marble halls,

and have second lines like this:

> With vassals and serfs at my side.

Someone has to scrub the marble, it follows as the day the night. And scrubbers like to dream, too.

V. REVENGE

Jason: O, my dear, dear children!
Medea: Dear to their mother, not to thee!
Jason: And yet thou didst slay them?
Medea: Yea, to vex thy heart.

Euripides,
MEDEA

As a vexer of hearts Medea has held the world title for twenty-five centuries. Betrayal by her husband Jason drove her to seek a vengeance so terrible—the murder of their two sons—that it remains an outpost of horror in our imaginations. Its message underlines an important life skill: Beware whose toes you step on, whose power you poach on. Take care whose pride you injure, whose well-being you threaten. You are courting one of the most savage of our instincts: revenge.

Who among us has not had a fantasy or twenty of getting back at someone who, fairly or unfairly, got the best of us? If our wits or fists fail us at the crucial moment, our imaginations rarely fail us moments later. Our honor and self-esteem smarting, we fantasize getting the last word, or assaulting and battering our way back to equilibrium. If we're lucky, our fantasies, however violent, can eventually cool us down.

If we stay hot, things usually just get hotter. It is a matter of record that most murders are committed by persons known to the victims. Revenge is a common motive. Wars, terrorism, feuds, duels, and trials are other bitter consequences of our inability to get our temperature down when someone drives it up. We hunger, we thirst, we burn for revenge, to hear it told. Of our primal instincts, it is prime. And civilizing it isn't easy.

One of the most difficult to follow of Jesus' teachings is his urging that we turn the other cheek. Within the ethical system that he preached it is perfect wisdom, a check to our natural bent to get down and wallow with our adversary. But for most of us painfully inching our way to a state of grace, it is the stricture most likely to trip us up, the banana peel on the stairway to paradise.

Not hitting back makes us look bad. *Weak.* Hitting back feels good and looks good. Especially if we can hit back harder than we were hit. But if revenge is an equalizer, it is a grim one. And deep down most of us know that to pursue it is to make a bigger mess than it's worth.

Montaigne, in his essay on cruelty, observed:

> It seems to me that virtue is something other and more noble than the inclinations to goodness which are born in us.... He who, from a natural sweetness and easiness, should despise injuries received would do a very fine and a very laudable thing; but he who, provoked and nettled to the quick by an offense, should fortify himself with the arms of reason against the furious appetite of revenge and after a great conflict finally master it would doubtless do a great deal more. The first would do well; the latter virtuously.

In Montaigne's eyes, Michael would be a man of virtue.

Michael

"The first thing I did was buy two gallons of quick-drying porch enamel. I knew what street he always parked his car on, and I knew that it would be absolutely deserted at three or four in the morning. The first dry night that came along, I put the paint cans in a shopping bag, walked the seven or eight blocks to his street, and found his car, a new Volvo.

"The street was quiet. I had already loosened the tops of the paint cans. I lifted them out of the shopping bag and poured paint over the car, slopping it into any hole or crevice that looked like it might lead to something vital. I had brought along a package of navy beans in case his gas cap had no lock. It didn't, so in they went.

"Several blocks away I popped the empty paint cans into the top of a garbage can that had been set out for early morning pickup. A few minutes later I was home and in bed, chortling away.

"But it wasn't enough. It just didn't give me real satisfaction. A few nights later I was in my car heading for the wilds of Connecticut where my ex-partner's summer home was. It was isolated and easy to get into without being seen. I had brought along some cans filled with gasoline. I splashed gasoline around all through the house and headed for the back door.

"I lit a wad of paper, threw it in, watched the fire get started and hightailed it out of there. By the time I drove through the nearest town, the fire alarm was sounding."

Michael, some years ago, had gone into business with a friend who had put up all the money. The business had been Michael's idea, and he had planned to pay back his share of the money from his first profits. The business was profitable, but his partner, in brief, had found a loophole in their agreement, and forced him out in humiliating circumstances.

"I was absolutely floored. I felt hurt, betrayed, outraged, every kind of bad thing all at once. I had little money, only the promise of things to come—which now weren't coming—so I had to scramble for a job. I was so stunned, the only thing I could think of was revenge. I thought of beating the hell out of him, which I could have, and I spent hours fantasizing all kinds of brutal confrontations.

"Then I got into all those fantasies about throwing the paint on the car and burning down his house in Connecticut. But the hang-up there was the fact that I would be the first person they'd check out. The one with a hot motive. Which made me even madder. However careful I was, I'd still be suspect number one. And I didn't think I could do any of those things anyway. And that didn't help either.

"What made me even madder was that I was behaving like a martyr, and taking the high ground. 'Let it be on his conscience,' I thought. Big deal. But the truth was we'd had a few altercations before this one, and I had tried to talk it out. But this time I thought, 'The hell with it.'

"I think the fantasies helped in that they gave me the illusion of getting back, as though I were seriously planning, and would carry out those plans, to get even. But as I went along and saw both the danger of doing what I was planning and the likelihood that I really couldn't carry it off, I think it added to the frustration, added to the feeling of really having been *had*. So in the long run they didn't get me over the deep anger I felt.

"I began talking over the situation with friends, and they all sympathized with me, which didn't help the martyr bit. Some of them said I should sue, which I didn't know much about. Others said I should just forget about it and go on. But one of them, a guy who worked in Wall Street and had a lot of offbeat connections said to me, 'You ought to pay somebody to break that guy's legs. I know somebody who can set that up for you if you want to do it.'

"Well that opened up a whole new fantasy horizon, particularly when he told me who could arrange it because it was somebody I knew. He was a very colorful character who owned a bar downtown where my Wall Street friend and I had been many times. Well, the prospect was delicious because it offered a way to get back without getting blamed for it. It could look like a mugging or something. Well I thought about that for days, particularly the leg-breaking part.

"To make a long story short, I finally got it up and dropped by the bar one night, and thought I'd mention something about it to John, the owner. Well, we got into it, and he asked did I want to go all the way or just break a few bones. And I said the latter, and he said it could be arranged for about five hundred dollars.

"And I said, well, I wanted to think about it. I remember him saying that if my ex-partner was such a bastard, I should get him, that I shouldn't be a softy. And he had looked at me as though I was one. Which didn't help me with my feelings about myself at that time, either. Well, I went home and I thought about it, and in a minute I just started laughing and laughing, probably for the first time since I'd left the business. I had gotten *that* close to the juiciest kind of revenge, and I knew that wasn't what I wanted at all. I didn't want to hurt anybody that way ever. And I began to feel better.

"And that was kind of a turning point. I knew I had to accept that I had been beaten. And if I was to salvage anything at all out of it, I had better learn something from it. But I think the thing that still bothered me most was that I hadn't tried to save the situation by talking it out with my partner. I turned that off when I convinced myself it wasn't worth talking out. I didn't want to be involved with people who would do that kind of thing. I had simply trusted the wrong man.

"But I couldn't put it down that easily. And I remembered what some of my friends had said about suing. I started having some big fantasies of courtroom drama, the jury viewing me as the poor injured innocent, and my partner as some kind of archfiend. And suddenly this vision of a stunning victory in the halls of justice took over.

"I got a lawyer who said I had a case, and we sued. But the lawyer proved pretty much a dud, and I didn't like the way it all dragged on and kept all that bad feeling stirring around inside me. I thought about it so often it made me sick. And I thought after a while that this suing business was just making it worse. I had a good new job, and I wanted just to get off to a fresh start and forget it.

"I told my lawyer to settle it now and get it over with, and we finally settled before the trial for a token amount, which I think the lawyer took half of. It was a mess on top of a mess as far as I was concerned. And I got back to the point where I felt I had to face the fact that I had lost. My picture of myself as a winner was pretty tarnished. So I thought it would be better to be a learner than a loser. I was still in my late twenties, and I thought there might still be some hope," he laughed.

I asked Michael what, if anything, he concluded from his experience.

"Several things. You should be careful who you get in bed with. Business is business, and money is money and it does funny things to people. Some folks out there will screw you or kill you for a nickel. And that's scary. But it's good to know. You just have to be careful, and not be a sap. I tried to look at things, too, that I might have done to bring all this on. That helped, because I found some things that helped me grow up a bit. Things about attitude and handling people—and myself. I remember thinking: 'He must have done this to get revenge on *me*. But why? Or was it just the money?'

"I think the most valuable thing that happened in the long run was that I learned I wasn't as smart as I thought I was, that I did have a lot to learn. And I learned. Grin and bear it, I believe it's called."

In *Structure and Function of Fantasy*, Eric Klinger concluded that although "fantasy is incapable of reducing drives," it "can prevent or reverse the build-up of anger." For Michael fantasy worked like an escape valve for the anger and frustration that boiled up from his injured feelings and his sense of injustice. The primitive scenes of revenge that raced through his mind also bought him the time to cool off and try to cope more rationally with his dilemma. As Jerome Singer, quoted in an article in *Vogue* (November 1976), phrased it: "Usually by the time we have finished daydreaming of humiliating, scolding, perhaps even punching our adversary, we are over our rage, and can deal with the real situation more sensibly."

Michael did not have an easy time of it. His anger was ferocious. His feelings of hurt and injustice were compounded by his fears of having contributed to the problem, and his shame in having reacted to the attack in perhaps too "soft" a manner. Only when he tested the reality of his violent intentions with John at the bar and laughed at them did he begin to come out of the clouds.

Suing his partner probably helped remove some of the stigma he might have felt about being a "softy," but as time wore on he tired of it, realized that it continued to stir his anger and frustration, and abandoned it for a fresh start.

Had Michael been less stable, his partner could have been in for trouble. Acts of revenge have filled police blotters for years. Buildings have been burned, bones have been broken, reputations ruined and feuds fanned into flame, all in the hot pursuit of eyes for eyes and teeth for teeth. Hatfields and McCoys, Gallos and Bonannos, Lancasters and Yorks have filled our back streets and back roads with violence for aeons.

But, of course, revenge isn't always front-page news. In the humdrummery of our private lives, we flirt with it daily, and in our heads, at least, we give someone or other their comeuppance on a daily basis.

Madeline

"At work, when I'm feeling in an embattled, defensive situation, like now, when my raise is due and nobody is saying anything to me about it and I'm absolutely furious about it, there is a recurring daydream that takes over. I can feel my face turn sour, my insides go all lemony, and I know I'm going for revenge.

"I fantasize that some former boss or colleague who liked me, and is now in some powerful position, has just contacted me and put out feelers about a job. This person then proceeds to ask me to lunch and woo me ardently to come work with his or her company at a big step-up in salary. Obviously, I waste no time saying yes. When I get back to the office, I call my boss and tell him I want to see him right away. As I walk into his office, he greets me with a big smile, and says he had been about to call me in to tell me some good news.

"'Aha, I have some good news for *you*,' say I. Then I tell him about the new job and give my notice. At this point I am in *heaven*. And he is shocked. 'I was just about to tell you about your raise,' he says. I thoroughly enjoy the conversation that follows as he tries to get me to stay. Alas, he cannot meet my price and I exit, laughing to myself. Revenge is mine!"

I asked Madeline how soon, or if, she planned to talk to her boss about an increase. "Oh, I will. Probably in a few weeks. I have to get myself up for it." I told her that I had had similar fantasies in the past, and we both agreed this kind of daydream was highly satisfying—punishing others for not recognizing our obvious merit, particularly when recognition seemed overdue.

"It's the overdue part that usually gets me," Madeline continued. "It's so damned rude, to begin with. I mean we all understand the language. A raise means thanks and encouragement. No raise means either hard times or no confidence. No word either way can mean a variety of things, number one being that your boss is at the very least a bit of a sadist."

We agreed that the fantasy of a flattering new job offer helped ease the sting of rejection, or feelings of rejection, and helped overcome the uncertainties that we might not be doing such a great job.

"Now I know it's bothering me," Madeline continued, "or I wouldn't be daydreaming about it. I don't want to have to do the asking. It's so much more encouraging when they offer. But I'm going to have to ask. And it's going to cost them more this way."

The boss gets it coming and going. If he misses a cue, shock waves of anxiety and paranoia bounce off the walls. Sometimes what he does is worse than what he doesn't do. As Gene's fantasy illustrates.

Gene

"I'm stuck in the most incredible situation. My boss, who's head of sales, comes out on the road to work with me several times a year. We get along fine as far as the business part of it goes. No problems. I mean I'm one of the best producers the company has. I've got great relationships with my customers, and I get a lot of business out of my territory.

"So he really doesn't have to work when he's with me, and get on my ass like he has to with a lot of the other guys in the field. Well, as you know I'm divorced, and I've got friends I like to go out with on the road—buyers, secretaries, whatever—girls that I've met through business usually. So he has this image of me as a swinger, and when he comes out to work with me, which is more than he works with anybody else, he's out for fun. Big fun.

"And he expects me to pimp for him, or at least that's what it all boils down to. Wherever we go, and I know a gal, she has to drum up a friend. Which ordinarily I wouldn't mind. But he's obnoxious socially. He wants to do two things. Drink and score. And talk about both all the time, even when we're with the girls. As a matter of fact, especially when we're with the girls. And if he likes my date better than his, forget it. Mr. Drunk-with-Power just moves right in.

"Now the girls I usually see are not broads, which makes it a real problem. They're nice gals. I don't mean I don't score occasionally, but they're not pickups. And very often they're buyers or merchandise managers, people that I not only enjoy going out with, but who are important to me in business. So when he acts this way, he's not only abusing the social relationship I might have with the girl, he's jeopardizing any business relationship I might have. Which is what really kills me, because he's the sales manager, the guy who ought to be setting the standards, not acting like an ass. No class.

"Even if I'm entertaining a group of people—clients with

their wives—and he's along as the big vice-president from the home office, chances are he'll make a pass at somebody's wife. I tell you, I've lost customers, or had to spend six months wooing a customer back because of him.

"I don't know what it is. Maybe he's going through male menopause or something, because something's wrong, and I keep praying the company's finally going to get on his case and boot his ass out. He's one of these guys that some years ago sold his way to glory, snowed the president, got the big job, and is riding it for all it's worth.

"To top it all off, he's married and has six kids. Are you ready? Which you usually have to hush up, because a lot of gals just won't go for that. As a matter of fact when he comes out to work with me now, a lot of the girls I know don't want to go out with me if he's around, let alone drag a friend into it. And I usually have to wind up lying that I'm no longer seeing some girl he remembers from last time.

"I've tried to tell him in a low-key way what's bugging me, but it doesn't really sink in. It just seems to whet his appetite for more. The last couple of times I've been ready to let him have it, but then I think, 'You'll get canned. Or he'll screw you in some way. Forget it. He'll be gone tomorrow. Hang on.'

"I really need to stay about another year to establish my experience with the company, then I'm getting the hell out. *If* I can hang on. Till then, I just sit and fester about it.

"But my feelings about him are really so bad at this point, that I really want to get him. We have an annual sales meeting in New York, and usually John's wife comes in with him for shopping and shows and so on. So here's the fantasy:

"I would rent an extra suite in the hotel we were all staying at. And I would tell John in advance that I had him all fixed up with a chick on such and such a night. I would tell him to tell his wife he had to go to a special meeting or something and get himself free for a couple of hours. And the girl I'd have all lined up for him would be just some hooker.

"Then, on the side, I would tell John's wife that we were

arranging a little surprise presentation for John, but that he didn't know our plans, just that he was going to a meeting. And we thought it would mean a lot to him if she'd be there. I would tell her I'd pick her up in her room when everything was about ready, but not to let on to John what was up.

"That night I'd ask the hooker to take all her clothes off and get into bed just before John was due to arrive. John would arrive, and I'd send him into the bedroom. I'd tell him I had to leave for a couple of minutes to pick up *my* girl, and she and I would shack up in the living room of the suite. Then, when we were both finished, or wanted to take a break, we'd all have a drink together.

"Then once I was sure he was in bed and going at it, I'd go pick up John's wife, bring her down to the suite, and quietly let her in. I would hand her the sealed envelope with my resignation in it, tell her to go back into the bedroom and wait with everyone else, while I went out to get John to bring him in for his big surprise. Gotcha!"

I complimented Gene on his ingenuity, and he replied, "I've worked on it for months to get it just right. The only thing I can't make work right yet is being able to be in the bedroom when John's wife walks in. I've visualized the look on his face a thousand times, but if I ever tried to pull it off in real life, I couldn't be there. I'd be too much of a coward."

I asked Gene if he thought he could pull it off in real life.

"Never," he shot back, "in a month of Sundays. I could do it to him tomorrow, but I couldn't do it to his wife. I don't particularly like her, but I feel sorry for her. She's married to an ass and knows it and can't do anything about it, or won't. But I'll be out of it soon. She'll probably never get out of it. Unless she kills him. That I could help her with," he added with a laugh.

I asked Gene if he thought the fantasy worked for him, helped him in any way, and he said, "It has to. I've clung to it for dear life sometimes. I figure I can't, or won't, do anything about the situation, but thinking about getting revenge helps a bit. Sure. And I'll just keep thinking about it and improving on it probably until I leave the company.

"I don't always think the best thoughts about myself for not reading him out and quitting, but I've just figured it's to my advantage to put in my time and get out cleanly and with a good name. Nobody there will ever know what I really thought."

Of all of life's trials, few can be more frustrating than a conflict on the job that seems insoluble. A struggle with an equal, or with someone lower down in the pecking order can usually be resolved with some imagination and effort. But when the conflict is with the boss, our jobs can be on the line when we rattle the cage. And it always comes down to whether we can afford to leave *now*. If we've got plenty of mad money and our prospects for employment are good, we can thumb our nose at the boss and take our chances. If not, we may have to bide our time and wait for the cavalry to come to our rescue. Unfortunately, ulcers and migraine are usually camped a bit closer, and get to us first.

In Gene's case, matters are not so dire. As a "producer" he can get another territory with another company when he's ready. He wants another year for the record. He has decided he can hold out till then. And the knowledge that he can and will get out takes the pressure off.

Gene's fantasy takes the pressure off, too. But other pressures he feels—about leaving with a good name and hoping for a good recommendation—will probably deprive him of any chance of setting the record straight with his boss when he leaves. Like Michael, he will have "to grin and bear it." And get over it.

Occasionally, with a bit of inspiration, we can make our revenge fantasies come true, and work for us. As Connie did, with hilarious and happy results.

Connie

"What I really wanted to do was grow up, find myself, be stronger, smarter, more independent *and* hold on to Ken all at the same time. Which, if you had known me at the time, and Ken, you would have guessed could only happen with a brain transplant. Two brain transplants.

"I was the perfectly stifled wife and mother of two, and the first on my block to have my consciousness raised. Or *teased*, I think puts it more accurately. I had begun reading some of the Lib literature, and talking with some other women, and just looking around, and the whole thing caught my imagination in a big way.

"I think I overreacted, really, in the first blush of it all. If I had been a bit cooler about it, things wouldn't have gotten so out of hand. But there you are. No half measures for me.

"Given my hyper personality, I really needed other activities along with the housekeeping and child-rearing. I was good at both, and when I ran out of things to do, I invented all sorts of impossible projects. You know, like putting ruffles on the ruffles. And I began getting so nervous. By the time Ken got home I was still three feet off the ground. I think it affected everybody.

"Well, he had his hands full with me, and I with him. And I began with these fantasies of getting my master's in education and teaching, of being this brave-new-woman type with an approving husband and an admiring crowd of friends. 'Isn't Constance *wonderful*,' and all that. Which soon proved to be an illusion, because the minute I started talking seriously about it, almost everyone thought I had gone cuckoo. Including Ken, who was absolutely crestfallen.

"Nobody was ready for it, including, as it turned out, me. But once I got the taste of it, once I felt it could happen to me, I could make it happen, that was it. It was just as though death was this way, life was *that* way, and no doubt about it, I was going *that* way. And I really felt confident I could pull it off, that it would be all right—better than all right—great, if everybody would just relax and let me do it.

"Our crowd were pretty much all young, well-to-do, on-the-way-up types, with the going-places husband, and the happy wife who stayed at home. None of the women worked, or thought about it. It just wasn't done.

"Ken was buffaloed by the whole thing, thinking

something was wrong with him that would make me want to get out of the nest. I don't think he was against it so much as he just wasn't sure how to handle it.

"Anyway, here we were: I was just exploding; he was just miserable. Now that I look back, I think I was pretty awful. I was just so full of myself, I was obnoxious. And Ken began to get surly, much more critical of how the house was being run than he ever was before I began studying, very unsupportive as far as my progress with my courses was concerned. I just couldn't seem to get him into thinking of me as anything other than the role model for domestic engineer. He was trying, but it wasn't working.

"Well, eventually it was icy silence. Then we thought we had better spend some time apart, and he moved out, both of us in tears. But all through this, I had this vision of myself as on my own—still a mother and a lover, but not stuck at home all day going crazy. And I believed in that vision. I remember fantasies of myself as the inspiring and beloved Mrs. Chips. Well, anyway, Ken moved in with his younger brother in his bachelor apartment and that was that.

"I kept hoping he would reflect on things, accept what I wanted to do and jump on the bandwagon. I had tried to convince him that our relationship in the long run would be much stronger if I felt better about myself and what I was doing. Well, in the meantime he would come over to visit the children, and I'd either be out or off someplace by myself studying. Sometimes he would take them out.

"But a lot of times, especially if I were out, he would stay at the house, dig into the food, make a horrendous mess in the kitchen, feed the kids in about three different rooms, and leave it all for me to clean up. I couldn't believe it, but he did it. I think he just wanted to keep his hand in. To let me know he wasn't coming around. The other thing he did really blew my mind.

"As it turned out, one of the regular nights he came to see the kids was just before my usual washday. And although he never asked, never said one blooming thing about it, he would bring over his little bag of laundry and leave it for me to do. And I, like an idiot, would do it.

"Well, I kept on doing it. But, of course, it was a mistake. I got madder and madder at myself. And what was happening was that even though we separated to think it over, supposedly, he was not so subtly telling me he wasn't thinking, he was just waiting for me to give in, give up.

"At least that's the way I took it. And it was doubly frustrating, because I had been so sure I was going to win, that I could have my way and keep Ken, too, that it would all work out and we'd both be so much happier. Lots of tears, I'll tell you. Because I felt I was going to lose him. I just wasn't giving up my goal.

"Well the more the dinner messes and the laundry went on, the more I saw it as pure antagonism. And though I tried to pass it off, be blasé about it to myself, it really began to grind on me. Finally it got me into a rage. And then I began fantasizing about how I would get back at him. Of course, the first thing I thought was going right for divorce, having the papers served, the whole bit, and getting it over with.

"But I just couldn't. I didn't want a divorce. The scenes would go through my head of Ken and me and the children all going separate ways, and I couldn't stand it. But I felt I had to make some kind of stand. I thought if I could just find some kind of gesture that would get the point across without a big ugly scene, maybe we could get back to the table, so to speak.

"I got rid of the dinner mess by working through the children—'Clean up your mess, put the dishes in the dishwasher, don't leave them for me,' and all that—and that worked reasonably well. But the laundry was the problem. I fantasized all kinds of ugly speeches that I think would have just driven us further apart.

"And then I thought of it. I don't remember whether it was an idea of my own, or something I had read, or heard about or whatever, but I just loved it. It was so funny. It had everything. It was nonviolent. Symbolic. And a howl. I daydreamed about it over and over again. And it gave me a laugh every time. I finally decided to do it.

"The next time he dropped his laundry off, I did it, did an especially neat job of folding the towels and T-shirts and rolling the socks. And before I folded up his shorts, I sewed up the fly of each pair of them with about a dozen rows of stitches.

"Well, I spent most of the next week giggling to myself, envisioning his reactions. I saw him angry, furious. I saw him baffled. I saw him laughing. But when he called to cancel his next visit with the children, he said nothing about it and got quickly off the phone.

"Which took the edge off the joke, of course, and began to get me nervous. Score one for him. But then the next week he called me, was very pleasant, and said he wanted to take me out to dinner and talk. And this . . . exhilaration welled up in me that I had won, rather, *we* had won. It was the most wonderful night of my life, I think.

"He asked how the book work was going, what I hoped to teach, how soon I'd be ready, and I told him. We talked about some of the practical problems involved in my working—things affecting the children mostly. We fenced a little back and forth, but we really didn't need to. We both knew what was going on. Sooner or later I maneuvered my way into asking how he felt about things. 'Let's do it,' he said.

"So we did it. He moved back the next day. He brought me a gift, a beautiful gold bracelet. I dashed right out the next day and got him a gift: a dozen pairs of shorts. He roared and we laughed about it for weeks. I finished school, got a job teaching, and we've both been happy as clams ever since.

"It's quite a drill sometimes, of course, trying to touch all the bases. But together we've been touching them. We're both like new people."

Sometimes a little revenge works wonders, but few of us could carry it off with Connie's aplomb. For most of us, it is a game that can have no winner, an enterprise that works best for us in our fantasies, which can gratify us just enough to allow our better natures to rally their forces.

Connie's rich imagination is one of her greatest allies. It

helped her sense her dilemma and envision her way out. But her commitment to that way out threatened a part of her life—her marriage and family—that she wanted to preserve. Once again her imagination helped her find a subtle, albeit risky, gesture that provided a turning point in her relationship with her husband.

Without fantasy she might still have been "three feet off the ground," as she described her condition before going back to school. And she may have given in to the hostile feelings that developed during her separation from her husband, and moved toward a divorce that she really didn't want.

In an article in *Psychology Today* (July 1976), Jerome Singer suggested that

> those who have trouble using fantasy to enrich their experience or as a substitute for aggression run the risk of serious trouble at each stage of their lives. . . . The risks of an undeveloped fantasy life may include delinquency, violence, overeating and the use of dangerous drugs. . . . A well-developed fantasy life seems to be partly responsible for independence, tranquillity and realism. . . . A good imagination may inhibit impulsive and aggressive behavior.

Certainly a good imagination can help us curb our worst instincts and show us a better, more civilized way to handle the aggressive, unfair behavior of others. In matters of revenge the best advice may indeed be, "Do put off till tomorrow what you might do today." By then you will handle it better. You may even recall that ancient bit of wisdom that the noblest vengeance is to forgive.

VI. GLORY

Curtain up,
Light the lights,
We got nothing to hit but the heights.
Stephen Sondheim,
"Everything's Coming Up Roses"

And remember: Hit the heights before the heights hit you. They can be murder. Rooms at the top are hard to come by, even harder to hold on to. Management encourages a steady turnover.

But does that deter us? No. Glory is so seductive. Many of us would trade our shadows for one night of popping flashbulbs. Never mind what morning will bring. Tonight we *live.*

We want to be a football hero. A rock star. Miss America. Mr. President. Prima donna. *Numero uno.* Whatever it takes, we've got it. And we can do it. Clamber up the World Trade Center tower. Swim in a shark cage. Write a sequel to *Gone With the Wind.* Balloon across the Atlantic. Fly to the moon. Clone ourselves. Whatever. We will do it.

And if we don't? Well, if we survive, we can always fall back on the simple life. If you call that living. No press conferences. No gold statuettes. No talk show appearances. Why doesn't anybody ever do a feature story on runners-up? Was Vince Lombardi right? Is winning the *only* thing?

Win a few, lose a few is probably more like it. Just ask
Napoleon. On glory's road, you pass this way but twice.
Going up and going down. *Sic gloria transit mundi.*

But before the glory of this world does pass away, most
of us would love to have it pass our way, even for one brief,
shining moment. Price is no object. Give us a turn in the
spotlight. Music, maestro. *Please.*

Guy

"The magic moment arrives. The award for Best Actor.
Elizabeth Taylor, last year's winner of the Best Actress
award [in Guy's fantasy], is the presenter. There is a roar of
applause for her as she makes her entrance. She makes a
few opening remarks, then moves quickly to read the list of
nominees.

"The list is impressive. Olivier, a few others, and me,
nominated for my first starring role in a picture. Miss
Taylor asks for the envelope. There is deathly silence. 'And
the winner is . . .'

"*Me!* The orchestra strikes up the theme music from my
picture, and the audience goes wild with applause. I lope up
to the stage, carrying with me the Oscar I had won a few
moments before for Best Supporting Actor.

"I have just made Academy Award history. Two acting
awards in one evening. And it's all the more astonishing
because I only began my acting career a couple of years
before [in his fantasy] when I was fifty.

"It is total triumph. Me. The biggest winner ever. I make
a short speech, and at the end, hold both awards over my
head with a big smile. And I think of that pose as the one
that will be in all the newspapers."

To get to glory from here, chances are you're going to
have to cross Sunset Boulevard. Hollywood and its
environs remain a hotbed of upward mobility, a proper
place to get yourself good and deified. And nowhere does
glory shine about more intensely than in those heavenly
auditoriums where the Oscars are annually dispensed.

Being a movie star these days doesn't have quite the flash of being a media star, but no one can deny that being a movie star *and* getting an Oscar is to be dipped in gold. To have the opportunity to thank your mother and father in front of millions, or rattle on about the Indians and the PLO, or, even better, to be gloriously conspicuous by refusing to attend your own deification, is to see the Big Dipper.

Small wonder if those of us forced by circumstances to live on Main Street have an occasional fantasy of thanking everyone who made us possible. But to be able to thank everybody twice on the same night is really doing it up.

Guy is a successful and creative businessman, gregarious and outgoing. I was introduced to him at a party as someone who had just begun work on a book about daydreams and fantasies, and he immediately said, "I have a fantasy you might enjoy hearing," and he proceeded to relate his Academy Award story. I did not have the opportunity to talk with him at great length about it, but he did indicate it was a fantasy that recurred reasonably often, made him euphoric, and that the euphoria would often linger some moments after the vision of his triumph had faded.

I was moved by the spontaneity of his offering, which struck a theme that was to recur often in my conversations with others, that of aspiring to the kind of demigodhood that Hollywood concocts to perfection. No small part of its attraction is that as performers pretending to be others we are inevitably ourselves and, if successful, adored for just being ourselves. Adored, followed, touched, worshiped. Riches and fame can follow and, if our charms prove durable, immortality, too.

Few of us dare to set out on the path to that well-lighted Olympus, but we will line the path and cheer along the hardy souls who try, and occasionally give the hook to the unsuitable. And occasionally fantasize that it is we who make it to the top.

Our dreams of glory spring from many sources. Insecurity. Disappointment. Boredom. Frustrated feelings that we have not yet touched some point of distinction we had hoped for. Hopeful feelings that it isn't over yet, that there's still something of value realizable within the present framework of our lives.

Perhaps, having already subscribed to the practice of making human gods, we collect dividends when we identify with them in our fantasies. Having seen how our screen heroes and heroines go through their paces, we can steal a bit of their thunder by vividly imagining ourselves in their shoes. In this sense, then, we don't steal it. We've already paid for it.

We elect our fantasy makers, expect them to come up with fantasies we can use, and reward them handsomely when they do. We want something larger than life, not too big, not too small, but just right, something to cheer us up, make us forget, give us hope, perhaps even inspire us to rekindle our efforts to do something a bit more with our lives.

Of course, it isn't all Hollywood. We've torn up a lot of turf the world over following our dreams of being the best, the first, the most, the biggest, the smartest. We have sought and found glory in, on, and around our temples and battlefields, palaces and academies, laboratories and concert halls, parliaments and playing fields. Preceding, often directing the action are fantasies of achievement and conquest, of holding sway in the dominions of the mind, the heart, and the body.

Our fantasies of heroic accomplishments, of glorious pursuits are linked to the heroic myths that have been part of most of our earthly cultures. Men and women favored by the gods, touched by magic, capable of superhuman feats, relate us to perfection, set lofty standards, inspire us to hero worship. The myths themselves express our need for an intermediary with divinity, one capable of walking on earth and on air.

The heroes of our myths are usually more than just charismatic individuals, they are saviors and champions as well. In real life, as well as in myth and fantasy, we give special honor to those who have devoted themselves not to personal triumph, but to the service and salvation of those of us in need. Our lists of saints and martyrs, champions and defenders are filled with the names of those who attained glory tending to the needs of others.

If the Academy Award symbolizes the cult of the self, a hero's medal symbolizes the cult of the selfless. Stewart managed to get into both clubs in his fantasy.

Stewart

"When I was a kid I flew a lot, especially in small, private planes. And I loved it. Older cousins, and friends of the family had been in the Air Force in World War II, and when they got out after the war was over I think the first thing most of them did was get a Piper Cub. I was the kid everybody wanted to give a thrill. I remember always being excited and appreciative when they would take me up.

"My later flying experiences with commercial flights were all enjoyable, and I always looked forward to them as special events. Until I was in my early thirties, and got myself caught up in a neurotic siege that took me some time to sort out. One of its manifestations was this high nervousness and anxiety that would grab hold of me when I was flying, particularly, of course, during takeoff and landing, and during turbulence of any kind.

"At the time I had similar anxieties when I was in an automobile and someone else was driving. It was all part of this very troubled phase where I had these hyper fears of death and disaster.

"Coping with it wasn't easy, particularly when my job required fairly frequent flying trips. It was white knuckles, nervous sweats, and all that. Tranquilizers and martinis would help, but the agony was always there. And a big part of it, until I later understood some of the reasons for my problems, was the bad image it gave me of myself as this threatened, quivering idiot.

"During that year or so of bad times, two fantasies started developing. One of them I still enjoy. The other I still think of every time I fly.

"The first one started during a very turbulent flight in one of those small forty- or fifty-passenger jets they use for pond-jumping. We were at low altitude, ducking in and out of a storm, and I was reaching down to my toenails for something to hang on to. All at once I got this feeling of being in a motorboat in choppy water, or being in a jeep on a bumpy road, or being on some crazy amusement park ride where the jumps and the bumps are supposed to be part of the fun.

"We were flying just low enough, and slow enough, and the plane seemed to be skipping and bobbing through it all so easily and unthreateningly that the whole image worked. And bit by bit I began to relax, and actually enjoy it. It took some doing, but I imagined myself going on a very fast fun ride, that I was really getting my money's worth, and the thing to do to get the most out of it was to just *go* with it.

"And that image began working for me more and more. The thing that really helped it most was that the image seemed so sensible. You really do bump around in the air—hitting occasional gusts and updrafts and downdrafts and air currents and wind shears—in somewhat the same way you bump around on an old back road. And it's really not any more or less threatening.

"I don't think it ever made me wish for turbulence, but I did find the fantasy, the image of myself on this expensive joyride, just riding the winds for all I was worth, very easy to slip into. It got me through a lot of bad times. I remember specifically trying to recall the exhilaration I had felt on roller coasters, and some of those early flights with my cousins where they'd bank it and roll it and do all kinds of crazy things I just loved.

"Once my overall anxieties began to fade and I relaxed and got over most of my problems during that period, with the help of some counseling, my fears of flying subsided, too. But I still have that fantasy of having a ball when the going gets rough.

"The other fantasy is big. And it's glory all the way. I still think of it every time I get on a plane and get settled down for the flight. I don't . . . experience it any longer, but I think of it, and usually with a chuckle.

"As I said before, my fears of flying concentrated on the turbulent periods and on landing and takeoff, which of course are the two points in a flight when accidents are most likely to happen. And I really did it to myself. I was so sure something was going to happen that I would go to great lengths to check weather reports and arrive extra early for my flight so that I could get a seat by the emergency exit, or in the tail section.

"When you did read of a crash and there happened to be any survivors, they were usually sitting in the tail section. So there I would be, either next to the emergency door, touching the handle, memorizing the instructions, or sitting in the very last seat in the rear, which was a riot because in the rear of the plane you bounce around much more during a flight than up front. Like I said, I really did it to myself. And all the time I was clutching the armrests reading myself out for being such a big baby.

"I would torment myself with visions of crashes: in the jungle, in the mountains, in the ocean. I remember a trans-Atlantic flight I made sometime back before jets took over, and long before all the trouble I had with flying. I think the plane was a four-engine Constellation, and the crossing took hours and hours.

"I was quite young at the time and I remember vividly reading one of those pamphlets they put in the pockets in front of you. It was called, 'How to Ditch Without a Hitch.' It gave all this cheery information about what you should do if the plane should have to come down in the water. I mean it told you all the things you were supposed to do with rafts and flares, and how to get into your life vest and crawl out on the wings. It all seemed so colorful. And I remember it prompted fantasies of this big crash at sea.

"Well, when I later developed all this fear of flying, I would remember all of that and start daydreaming about this awful crash at sea with the flames, and the rafts and the burning oil slicks and the icy North Atlantic.

"And then I would envision these crashes on the runways at takeoff, and the plane would split open and burst into flame and we'd be out in this field, or all over some highway. It got to the point where I would actually time our takeoff, and if the wheels didn't leave the ground and the plane nose upward within the time I thought it should take, I'd start bracing myself for a crash.

"Soon after I started having all these fears and fantasies, I began putting myself into the picture, as a survivor, of course. You know, there I was right by the emergency exit. I'm out before the flames hit. But then I turn heroic. I immediately start rushing into the wreckage to pull people out before everything explodes into flame. I rush in again and again, pushing myself beyond my limits, hauling out two at a time. Finally my own clothes have begun to catch fire, and as I am bringing out the last that can be saved, I collapse.

"I come to in a hospital bed, just like in the movies, and people are all around talking in hushed tones. Then bit by bit things brighten up and I go through all these scenes of newspaper headlines calling me a hero, and TV newsmen pressing me for interviews, and being presented with medals.

"The things got so real that sometimes I'd be halfway to Pittsburgh before I even knew we had taken off. Well, that's exaggerating, but I really could get lost in them. I'd vary them: crashes at sea, crashes on land, terrible crashes, mild crashes, but always two things would happen. We would crash, sure enough. And I would become a hero."

Our imaginations, our abilities to fantasize often have to work overtime to help us with our fears, to help us acquaint ourselves with our dread, and, hopefully, overcome it. Stewart used imagery and fantasy to help him get over his extreme nervousness during turbulence and to guide him to a common-sense acceptance that what was really going on was not all that threatening.

His crash fantasies possibly worked in a way similar to Pat's rape fantasy (chapter III) in that it offered two benefits in one. Pat's fantasy helped her acquaint herself with, and calm her fears of rape, and allowed her to indulge in thoughts of guilt-free sex with a partner other than her husband.

Stewart's fantasies helped him face his fears of an air crash, taming them somewhat by his visions of not only being a survivor, but being a hero, which helped him over his guilt at being "such a big baby." Having seen the worst, and having worked his way out of it gloriously, he was on the road to immobilizing, hopefully overcoming, his fears. In this view, fantasy is not merely an unfortunate by-product of neurosis, an obstruction to life, but an instinctive and valuable tool to help the obstructed person face, endure, and overcome his or her blocks.

I asked Stewart if he had any doubts or feelings about his courage and bravery, or lack of it, and whether or not there were other fantasies in his collection that featured heroic acts on his part.

"I do remember a recurring fantasy when I was a kid about jumping off a cliff into the water to rescue someone who was drowning. There was a storm and the water was rough, and I managed to pull the person out of the water and struggle up onto the shore, and then sort of pass out. And when I came to I would blurt out, 'How did I do it? I can't even swim!' And everyone, including myself, would be in awe."

As we talked, Stewart said that as a child he had been afraid of the water, and had not learned to swim until he was in his mid teens. Even then fantasy was at work to help him cope with his fears of the water, and to help him with his guilt and insecurity about not learning to swim.

"As far as the bravery part goes, I've never thought of myself as courageous in obvious ways. I have tended to shy away from violence, and big tests of courage. When fears and suspicions of cowardice creep in, I can usually rationalize them away. I do think I have courage down deep. But I've never been a showboat. I don't look for opportunities for heroism. If one should come along, who knows what would happen? I just hope I would respond sensibly. I don't want to be a live coward. But I don't want to be a dead hero either."

At one point in his life, perhaps two, when his confidence and self-image were in doubt, Stewart would have liked to be a live hero—if his fantasies tell us anything—a man who could summon superhuman strength and make a lavish display of it when the opportunity presented itself.

Whether or not glory pays us a visit, we care about finding our own sense of worth, an identity acceptable, even appealing, in our own eyes and in the eyes of others. A good image of ourselves and our abilities is a kind of low-key glory, and one most of us seek.

We can find such glory in a skill, an activity, a calling. And as we progress in that chosen activity, the sense of self we find "showing our stuff," "doing our thing," gives us pride, perhaps even a ruffle and a flourish of glory. Our sense of who we are depends much upon our knowledge of what we can do, and a growing awareness, illuminated by a fantasy or two, of what *more* we can do.

Sometimes our call to "glory" comes early. In Evelyn's case it did. And it has carried her far.

Evelyn

"The greatest thing that ever happened to me happened almost sixty years ago when I was a young girl of nine or ten. By then I was an accomplished swimmer. And one summer—I think I was about nine—it just began to happen that wherever I was swimming, in a river or a lake or a swimming pool, people would gather around to watch me as I dived and swam, and would say, 'Oh, how wonderful she is.'

"It was so thrilling to me. I'll never forget the feeling it gave me, of having approval and admiration. I had had a very unhappy early childhood. I had been small for my age, and sickly, and because of family difficulties and problems, I had been farmed out to foster homes and boarding schools until I was about nine.

"But then in a boarding school, when I was five or so, I learned to swim. I just took to it naturally, and loved it so much that I spent every moment I could in the water. It seemed to be the one thing that gave me happiness, that made me forget my feelings of being unwanted.

"Of course, as I stayed with it, I got good at it. So by the time I was nine or ten, as I told you, people began to compliment me and encourage me, swimming became synonymous with good feelings about myself. And about the only good feelings I had.

"Well as school went along I improved as a swimmer, and soon I began to get involved in competition. I began as a sprinter, but my performances were only mediocre, and it began to depress me. Then, one day, I checked a middle-distance swim event by mistake, but entered it anyway. And won it. And from then on I became a middle- and long-distance swimmer, and I began winning championships.

"My self-image began to thrive, and I was able to put aside the insecurities and uncertainties that were still a part of me. When high school finished, I was offered a swimming scholarship to New York University.

"The Depression had hit, and it was clear that the only way I could hope to go to college was on a scholarship. But my mother was opposed to my accepting it. To begin with, her idea of college for women was to go one year only, find a husband, and forget it. Also, in those days, few women competed in athletics. For a woman to be going to college on an athletic scholarship was most unusual, and a bit unsettling for many people, my parents especially. And another important factor, I am Jewish, and, once again, in those days particularly, it was somewhat difficult for Jews to participate in, much less attempt to distinguish themselves in athletics. Well, the result of all these pressures was that I didn't accept the scholarship. But I wasn't vanquished that easily.

"Obviously I was a confirmed swimmer by then, but there's one other thing that came into play at this point that I neglected to tell you earlier. One of the boarding schools I had been sent to was the Ferrer School, one of the early progressive schools, where Will Durant taught, and where the Danas and Margaret Sanger and many other well-known people of that time were involved.

"Most of their curriculum was presented as a form of play. Of the many things they instilled in me I think the most important was that I must always try to think for myself and not try to become a part of the mold. So I had two things going for me at this turning point: I was a steady, buoyant, very competitive swimmer whose style everyone seemed to like. And I was a nonconformist. It wasn't too difficult to make the choice I did."

Evelyn's choice was to enter the world of amateur, and later professional, competitive and exhibition swimming. Her excellence in freestyle swimming was to take her across North and South America, and across Europe and the Middle East in the next fifteen years. From Canada to Brazil to Egypt to the French Riviera she broke records as a middle- and long-distance swimmer and built a collection of trophies, medals, ribbons, and citations, the overwhelming majority of them bearing words that translate into "winner."

In the 1940s Evelyn, now in her early thirties, was swimming in Cuba when Nazi submarines began to attack shipping in the Caribbean. "The war had finally reached out to us even there, and I knew it was time to go home."

She returned to the States, went to California, taught swimming and worked in an aircraft factory. When she returned to New York City, the war had ended, and a new kind of life opened up to Evelyn. She resumed her education at Hunter College, which had begun a program for "older women."

"The old competitiveness came back in a rush. I had to get A's, and I did." Following completion of her masters degree at New York University, she began teaching in the New York City public school system, swimming several times a week "to keep my form." She retired in the early 1970s, when illness, followed by two lung operations, made continuance of her career as a teacher uncertain.

"Why me? I kept asking myself," Evelyn continued. "I felt very angry, victimized. I had never smoked or drunk. I had lived a very healthy life. The same unhappy and bitter feelings I had had as a child rushed over me again. My strength had been depleted by the operations. I was one unhappy person.

"Then a swimming friend told me about a new program that the AAU [Amateur Athletic Union] had developed for swimmers in all age groups. Well, that rang the bell. My competitive juices started flowing. It sounded interesting."

Evelyn and I live on the same floor of our apartment building and swim in the same pool. About a month ago, having just returned from a trip to Toronto, she got on the elevator carrying her suitcase and a paper bag. With a little prompting she produced the contents of the paper bag—a gold trophy and a gold medal for her latest long-distance championship. "I did it," she smiled.

Two weeks later she returned from a marathon swim in the ocean at Atlantic City with another gold trophy. "It was so cold and the water was choppy," she declared. "They had to pull quite a few swimmers out of the water. Not me, thank God."

No indeed, not Evelyn. She is a champion swimmer again, back in form and style, traveling around the country, going for the gold. "Since I've been back at it, I've never won less than a gold medal," she admitted.

I asked Evelyn her feelings about winning and losing. "I can't accept coming in second," she said. "That's what I fight against, that's what I think about when I go the distance, that and concentrating on each stroke, making each one as good as I possibly can."

Training for competitive swimming, and the events themselves, can be grueling work, particularly for the long-distance swimmer. "What keeps you at it?" I asked Evelyn. "Is it the glory? The praise? The gold?"

"Well, remember I told you at the very start about that early moment in my life," Evelyn continued, "when I got all the praise and attention for my swimming. I don't think of that as glory, but it certainly was *shining*, and I loved it. But it really wasn't that part of it that got me going and kept me going. At least I don't think so. It's the pleasure I get out of doing something well.

"Really, there are so few things I think I do well—that's part of all that early insecurity, I'm sure. But I can swim. It's the best thing I do. It's . . . *me*!" And it's back in her life again in a big way. "Since my operations I feel a bit like damaged goods. But I'm swimming. And winning.

"I must say I do heave a sigh of relief now when I find out the competition won't be too great in an event that I enter. I never would have done that in the old days. And I have to admit there's another girl who's coming on strong in my age group. If I know she's competing, I will sometimes not sign up for the middle-distance events, where she could give me trouble. I stay with the long-distance swims, where I'm absolutely safe.

"I tell my doctors this and they laugh. They seem amazed at my recovery and my activity. They do tell me to relax more, swim to be swimming, not to put myself constantly under the strain to win. I understand what they're saying. But I can't accept it."

I asked Evelyn about her fantasy life. "I'm sure there were fantasies involved in that period I told you about when people first began to notice me swimming," she replied. "But then I *became* a swimmer. It's what I always wanted to do. And did.

"I always have fleeting images of finishing first, anticipating the good feeling it will give me. And I do have one all-encompassing illusion, I call it, that swimming will keep me young, keep me healthy, keep me from aging. And that fantasy, if you want to call it that, keeps me going.

"Also I think perhaps in another way I fantasize about swimming. Now, if I can see myself competing in an event, in Toronto or Atlantic City, or wherever, I know I can do it. And I do it."

Evelyn was fortunate to get inside her dream, follow it, and live it, and she is living it still. Whatever elements were at the root of her need to win, swimming, and winning at swimming, became her life and her glory. She is indeed a long-distance champion.

Evelyn's story points to a fact that most of us already know. Wherever we look, in every activity and enterprise in which we become involved, we can come up against those who not only have the talent and the gift to succeed, but the need and the determination to win, who will fight *not* to finish second. From this breed come our champions.

Among those champions are those who truly seem to be in it not so much for the personal glory and the acclaim, although they can accept these with simplicity, but because they so strongly identify with, and inevitably enhance and enlarge, those activities they undertake. From among these we elevate a select few to the status of hero.

To watch Pete Rose at bat, to hear him speak not of himself but of his team, the season, the game, to watch him season after season perform with strength and spirit and zest, is to identify him immediately with the sport, and to understand why commentators refer to him repeatedly as "Mr. Baseball."

In an interview during a recent telecast of a performance by the American Ballet Theatre, the young ballet star Gelsey Kirkland spoke admiringly of her colleague, Russian ballerina Natalia Makarova. When asked the sources of her inspiration, Kirkland, herself the subject of a recent *Time* cover and the brilliant new idol of dance enthusiasts, unhesitatingly cited Makarova, ending her accolade with the ultimate praise, "She *is* the dance."

Our heroes make us think, make us look to ourselves and our lives, excite us to fantasies of accomplishment and glory. If, in worshiping our heroes too much, we allow them to intimidate us rather than to inspire us to accomplishments of our own, we exalt them too highly and deny our own existence. And our fantasies, rather than fulfilling one of their roles as a call to resolution and action, can disintegrate into hateful reminders of our own inadequacy.

Fantasies can give us a design for living, but it is commitment and follow-through that gives us that all-important reason for living. And follow-through takes work. Day after day of it. But for those who *are* their work, their calling, their profession, it is a labor of love.

Evelyn trains every day in our pool. She is always the first one in the water in the morning. When my schedule permits a morning swim, and I pass through the gallery that overlooks the pool, I invariably look for her. When she is doing the backstroke, she is particularly easy to spot. Every stroke is perfect. And she is the only one in the pool who is smiling.

VII. DEATH

We're waltzing in the wonder of why we're here.
Time hurries by, we're here, and gone.
Arthur Dietz,
"Dancing in the Dark"

Gone where? That is the question. Of all of earth's creatures, we humans, it appears, are the only ones aware of our mortality. That awareness puts our imaginations to their ultimate test. If we're waltzing in the wonder of why we're here, we're hustling even more energetically to figure out exactly what happens to us in the hereafter.

Will we be born again? Or is this it? If we do come back, do we have to go through all this again? Or do we go on to something better? If so, how do we qualify? Is there a line? A test? A trial?

Answers to these and other questions have been handed to us many times in many languages. We have been so certain of some of those answers that we have gone to incredible lengths to ensure that all creatures here below are privy to, even subscribe to, the true way.

Whatever gospel, dogma, or personal conclusion we do subscribe to, one thing seems certain: It requires an act of imagination to envision that true way for ourselves, the better to weigh it in our hearts and minds, where, in time, we may summon the courage to believe and follow.

Even when we do imagine, and accept, and follow, and know the peace and direction these beliefs can bring to our lives, we can be tormented by doubt and fear. Can we hope for a full life? When our time comes, will we, in our own estimation, be ready? Can we, with grace, give up our friends and families to death? Can we endure, in Hamlet's words, "the heartache and the thousand natural shocks that flesh is heir to" without wishing for the end?

Can we, will we, indeed? If only we could know. For sure. It would all be so easy. We seek the truth. The best we can muster is wisdom, as in this, from the Upanishads:

> The sharp edge of a razor is difficult to pass over; thus the wise say the path to Salvation is hard.

The truth, and our salvation, lie somewhere beyond death, somewhere over the razor's edge. But that is undiscovered country. We have ground to cover here yet. And we keep death at bay as best we can. Even in our fantasies. Especially in our fantasies.

Death presented itself, in reality, to Edwin on a battlefield in France during World War II.

Edwin

"It felt as though the shell exploded right under me, it lifted me so far into the air. If it had, of course, I would have been all over France. As it was, it was close enough. So much raced through my mind. What happened? Am I alive?

"Well, I knew something had hit. And I remember vividly the thought going through my head that if I was able to ask the question, I had to be alive.

"But I couldn't see anything. I was terribly dazed. And I couldn't feel much. Then an image flashed through my head of the character from that antiwar novel, *Johnny Got His Gun* [by Dalton Trumbo], who was so horribly mutilated in battle. And I thought of myself being like that character, having to live the life he was faced with.

"I couldn't see at all. But bit by bit I came to, and became

aware of the sounds and voices around me. My platoon
sergeant was holding me. I was trying to touch, to feel my
face, and he kept pulling my hands away. And I remember
asking him, 'Are my eyes still in my head?' And he was
crying, and he said, 'I think so.'"

From his early youth Edwin had painted, and had
planned for a life as an artist. In the hospital, in the
darkness under his bandages, he feared and fantasized the
worst. "One of the things that tormented me most was
that vision of the hopeless life of the character from *Johnny
Got His Gun*. I knew that, thank God, all of my wounds
would heal, and I would be left whole. Except for my eyes.
The big question was, 'Would I be able to see again?'

"I imagined myself blind. I fantasized how I might live.
Who might take care of me. What I would do with myself. It
was shattering to think about. My greatest fear was that I
wouldn't be able to paint again. And that was agony. It
would be like a death. I would have to start all over again.

"Then this fantasy began developing that each day
absorbed more and more of my thought. I would write
scripts for radio. Make word pictures. It seemed perfect.
Not being able to see could actually be an asset. I could
concentrate purely on the images the words carried. I
began developing plots for dramas and mysteries. I saw
myself being at the studios during the broadcasts. Being
admired. Respected. Successful. I could hear the announcer
saying, 'by Edwin Green.'"

In time most of the sight returned to one of Edwin's
eyes. Radio's loss was painting's gain. He is well known
today for his watercolors and oils. He paints, exhibits, and
teaches in New York City, Maine, and Portugal.

Our fears of death, or the death of something or
someone precious to us, can haunt and torment us, and our
fantasies can rush in to show us the worst. And the way
out. Even when we neither see nor feel its imminence, as
Edwin did, we can have fantasies about our death and the
death of others. They can have, depending on each of our
lives, a multitude of sources.

We want life and love in abundance, and it is natural for us to fear their loss before we taste their fulfillment. If death perfects life by limiting it, surely we will stand closer to perfection with just one more opportunity to prove our worth.

When images of death haunt us, they arise like vapors from suspicions of our imperfection and our unreadiness to face whatever our views may be of a final judgment of our lives. The more they torment us, the more our self-image ails. Seldom can they be confused with a real wish for death. Much more they dramatize a wish for life. A better, more deserving one.

In the same way, when we envision the death of someone we love and by whom we are loved, we could be responding to our fear that we will lose the opportunity to more fully merit that love, to bring it closer to perfection.

Diana
_____

"One of my mother's favorite expressions was, 'Oh, you'll be the death of me yet.' She would say it in a kind of mock anger, rolling her eyes up to heaven, as though she wanted to be taken right at that moment. She would usually say it in reaction to something or other I had done that had displeased her or, to use another of her favorite expressions, 'exasperated' her.

"I remember her being very warm and loving. She could be playful, but also . . . expectant. Her 'you'll be the death of me' was usually reserved for moments when she was disappointed in me, and I knew it. It was almost always said teasingly, and followed with a pained smile, or a little laugh.

"But I remember it upset me to hear it. I loved my mother so much. And naturally I wanted her love, and approval, in return. I certainly didn't want to hear that my inadequacies would be the death of her, even in jest.

"I remember the thought of it troubled me even more when I began to have these fantasies of her death. I don't recall any images of how she died, mostly scenes of her being laid out in a coffin, and my being there, feeling very sad and guilty, feeling I had literally worried her to death. And I'll tell you I had one or two night dreams of seeing her in a coffin, which absolutely terrified me.

"Then to top it all, I remember seeing *Bambi*, the Disney picture, which almost killed me when the hunters shot Bambi's mother. Such a cruel picture. Really. I was in tears for days.

"I know all this sounds like I was a sad child. I wasn't. I was a very happy one, I think. This was about the only negative or worrisome thing I recall from my whole preteen period. And I think I exaggerate it in my mind now because of what was to happen.

"When I was fourteen my mother died in an automobile accident. And I'll tell you I was one desolate child. I was deeply troubled for months and months. I tormented myself with guilt about being responsible in some way for her death. And I thought that perhaps the daydreams I had about her death had meant that I wished for her death, and I was being punished for it.

"I thought of those night dreams of her death as being a kind of prophecy of what was to come, and my dreams began to frighten me. I thought of them—the content of them—as things that would come true. And then I began this whole syndrome of not wanting to go to bed, certainly not wanting to go to sleep. Who knows what I might see?

"Thank God my father was so good to me throughout the whole thing. I could have gotten into a very messy situation, I think. He was just so kind and supportive and reassuring. He wasn't analytical about it, he just said, 'Don't think those thoughts. Don't worry yourself that way. We have to get on with things.'

"And we did. And I pulled out of it, and got over it eventually. It wasn't until a couple of years ago when my father died, that I thought at length about that period of my life. I had a very clear picture of myself after mother's death trying to fight off the fear and the guilt that I had in some way been responsible for her death. I think it was the first time I consciously looked at, and understood, those fears as an adult."

There are other reasons that visions of death dance in our heads. There are moments we sincerely wish to see someone dead. They have hurt us. Or crossed us. Or they are merely in the way. Life would be just great if it weren't for them.

Claire

"When it became clear that my marriage was not going to work and that it was a mistake to go on with it, that nothing was going to make it right, I began dreading the inevitable confrontations, which I knew would be bitter and humiliating, and all the agonizing business of getting a divorce.

"There were regrets, and feelings of failure, but I think I had accepted these as unavoidable. In my mind I had already cleared away much of the debris. I wanted to get on with my life. My dislike for Roger had become so intense that I was afraid I would crack before I got free of it all.

"For a period of several months before we finally got down to it and got it over with, I had repeated fantasies of his death. I would usually arrange something remote, a plane crash somewhere, a phone call, a funeral, sometimes even a sizable insurance check to smooth out my new life. Roger traveled a great deal in his business, and spent a lot of his time flying. It seemed like the perfect solution.

"It got to the point that when I would hear the phone ring, a vision would spring into my mind of an airlines executive on the other end of the line telling me, as gently as possible, that Roger had been killed. I wouldn't be jubilant, but as the fantasy warmed up, the sense of relief, or release, would just sweep over me."

I asked Claire if any feelings of regret or guilt would occur during or after the fantasy. "No," she replied, "I don't think so. As a matter of fact I have a memory of looking for, waiting for those feelings. But they just never came. Which only strengthened my conviction that I wanted out. There were simply no feelings left.

"I knew in my heart of hearts, that I really didn't wish him dead. I was looking for an easy way out. If even for a moment, I wanted to feel the relief of not having to face the ordeal that I knew was coming. I'm afraid I was willing to try anything, in my mind, at least, to avoid a difficult time."

We can fantasize our own deaths, too, when things seem to be more than we can bear. If we were to eat little green worms and die, we could punish life, God, family, friends, enemies, creditors—any or all for pushing us into this dismal corner. Or just punish ourselves for being so pushable. Or just get *out* of it. Period. Punishment or no. If our self-image becomes so eroded, our sense of worthiness so damaged, death can seem to be the perfect out.

Our fantasies, then, can act for us as they do when we plot any revenge—help us examine just how far we *might* go if pushed, and buy us the time to cool off and pull back to a more sensible position from which to deal with our problems creatively. In the meantime we might indulge in a fantasy or two of just how we might do it, from overdosing on Seconal to taking an early evening stroll down the passing lane of the Long Island Expressway.

Mark

Mark (see chapter II) related fantasies he had in his late teens and early twenties when he was struggling with anxiety about his homosexual feelings.

"The fantasies had a definite pattern. I would be with my lover, my male lover. He would be someone I knew in real life, a friend or a passing acquaintance to whom I was attracted, but someone with whom I knew there could be no real, or at least no lasting relationship.

"In the fantasies, the relationship would be 'real' and lasting. And we would be killed. In an accident, or by some hostile act. Usually I would imagine our being in some exotic or romantic setting.

"In one of them, for instance, we would be driving along those twisting, turning roads along the Riviera, in a convertible, probably a Rolls-Royce, aware of being gloriously together, when suddenly a car would swerve toward us from the opposite direction, forcing us off the road and off a cliff into the Mediterranean."

I asked Mark if, in the fantasy, he dwelled on the moment of death, of the pain or struggle that might be involved. "No," he replied. "Never, that I can think of. Usually right away I would move on to the general reaction to our death—how it would be reported in the newspapers or television, what people would think. Would it be obvious that we were lovers? If so, what would they think about that? Usually, I think, the conclusion was that we were.

"There was another one I remember that was really like a movie adventure story, rather than anything that might be even remotely related to real life. We were being pursued by armed men. We were some kind of espionage agents, or resistance fighters, very heroic. The men pursuing us were definitely the bad guys. The Nazis, or whatever.

"However valiant our struggles, we would be trapped and shot, and we would die together as heroes. I don't think in that one there was any public worrying about whether we were gay or not. I guess it didn't seem to fit the picture. But I remember very poignant feelings about martyrdom and dying with somebody I loved."

As we talked about the fantasies, I asked Mark who the men were who died with him, and it appeared the fantasies were engineered to fit the type of man he cast in each one. His companion on the Riviera was, by his description, handsome and wealthy, someone who would fit quite naturally into a glamorous setting. His companion in the second fantasy was, in his words, "fearless, athletic, tough, kind of a Robert Mitchum type."

We agreed on several points about the fantasies. That the first one in particular indicated his desire to "come out" to the public, but only after his death. At that point in his life, Mark said, it would have been impossible for him to admit his homosexuality to anybody. He had needed to, he said, but couldn't. His daydream dramatized that need and the only possible way he felt it could be fulfilled at that time in his life.

It could also have allowed him to indulge in being "gloriously together" with someone with whom he could not hope to have a loving relationship. Death would come as a self-imposed punishment for indulging in a relationship that was unacceptable to him. Or as a judgment by a society he knew condemned and ridiculed homosexual love.

Many of us were brought up with the teaching that death itself is punishment for the wicked. With this in mind, knowing we have misbehaved, death cannot come to us, even in fantasy, as a friend. In the same way, if we are perfectionists, cannot accept our imperfections, and suspect we will be judged for them, we cannot face death with anything other than dread. If death comes as a punishment, if we feel we cannot pass judgment, we know we have lost our opportunity for salvation, a second chance, another life, a life in heaven.

What yawns before us then is nothingness. Or worse, hell. Our pictures of hell seem a good bit clearer than our notions of heaven. Dante's version of what happens to the souls of the proud, the gluttonous, the envious, the avaricious, the slothful, and other unworthies curls the hair.

Michelangelo's vision of *The Last Judgment* is not encouraging to any of us with a spotty record. With the possible exception of George Bernard Shaw, few artists have gone out of their way to calm our fears of going to hell. From the Bible to Bosch, from Doré to Disney, the picture isn't pretty. If hell is a conspiracy of fantasy makers, it signed up the best.

No wonder fears and anxieties about death and dying stir in the back of our minds, prompting some of our most engrossing fantasies. Nobody, but *nobody* wants to go to hell.

Jane certainly didn't. Her dream of it, and the fantasies that followed are a little like science fiction. Or perhaps detective fiction is more apt, because she tracked down the key to it years later. Or at least she thinks she did.

Jane

"This is too weird to tell anybody, but I'm going to anyway, mostly because of the answer I found years later. Or think I found. Anyway, whether you can use it or not, you'll get a laugh out of it.

"It all started with a dream, a night dream, I had when I was about eight or nine. To begin with, you should know I come from a very strong Protestant background, not severe, but lots of church activities and lots of talk of right and wrong, and good little girls going to heaven, and bad little girls doing the devil's work. And since I wasn't always a good little girl, you-know-who developed this thing about going to the blazes . . . wherever that was.

"Well, here's the dream. Oh, you should know I went to school in the country, and lived close enough that I could walk back and forth. Well, in the dream I was walking home from school one day and suddenly, not far from home, all hell broke loose. Literally. Right there in the middle of the road.

"The earth was all torn up, and everything was heaving and tossing around like in an earthquake. And there in the middle of everything, completely red from head to toe, with red horns, a red tail and a red pitchfork was the devil himself, with fire all around him, just waiting for me. And the really awful thing was he seemed to be just oozing out of this steaming heap of cooked tomatoes. They were all over the place, and suddenly I was in them and sinking in them, and he was heading toward me with his pitchfork.

"And, of course, at that point I must have awakened, screaming probably, because I have no memory of anything else happening. What happened in real life after that, not surprisingly, is that I developed this crashing aversion to eating tomatoes. I mean I think I would just get sick if I even saw them around, particularly the stewed ones my mother used to can and serve all winter long.

"That dream was so vivid, and affected me so violently that it haunted me for years. I fantasized about it constantly, with these fearful feelings. I remember for weeks after that I was afraid to walk home from school, and I had visions of getting to that point in the road where the dream had occurred, and thinking the devil was going to pop out at any moment with all those stinking tomatoes and all that fire and steam.

"It is one of the most memorable things of my childhood, and I don't think I could eat tomatoes for years after. I eat them now all the time, and occasionally when I'm looking down at them, I'll think of that dream, and howl.

"I think I have the answer to it. First, one more little point of background. My mother had always prepared the usual kind of southern home cooking. And we used to have large family get-togethers every few weeks at our house, or my grandmother's house, or one of my aunt's or uncle's homes. One of my aunts loved to try different kinds of cooking.

"I remember my father complaining bitterly whenever he knew we had to go to her house for dinner. The only memory I have of dinners at her house was one special one where she prepared all Chinese food, and served it with chopsticks, which I thought was very exciting, and I think I loved the whole thing.

"Well, anyway, a few years back, when I went home for a visit, my aunt invited the family over for dinner one night. And my aunt made a comment before she served the dinner. She said something like, 'I hope you're going to like what we're having tonight. I remember once when you were a very little girl that you took one or two bites and wouldn't finish it. It was probably too hot for you. But now that you're a grown-up New Yorker, I'll bet it's just your dish.'

"Well, I couldn't believe it. The dish was Shrimps Fra Diavolo, you know, shrimps in a hot garlicky tomato sauce. And she was right, I do love it. 'I didn't put a lot of hot sauce in it this time,' my aunt goes on, 'but here's the bottle if you want to add some more.'

"And on the table she points to a small red bottle of something called Louisiana Flame Sauce or Louisiana Hot Sauce, I can't remember which. On the label was this big luscious-looking red tomato, and right next to it stood this vicious looking cartoon of the devil, all in red, with red horns, a red forked tail and a big red pitchfork coming right at me.

"Now am I crazy, or was that it? It must have been. I must have hated the taste of the tomato sauce the shrimps were in, with all that hot sauce and garlic, saw that picture of the devil on the bottle, and gone bonkers someplace inside. From then on in, as far as I was concerned, the devil was in the tomato business, and I was having none of it."

When we are children we are especially vulnerable to the kind of disturbing association Jane made between the devil and the tomato, or hell and Shrimps Fra Diavolo. That kind of association has often been at the root of personality disturbances that may not surface as obvious problems until much later in life.

Jane has long since gotten over her aversion to tomatoes (and her morbid fear of hell, she told me), but an individual less healthy than she is might still be fighting the battle.

So much of our feeling about death depends on our feelings about life. If life feels good to us, and we are confident of our continuing sense of well-being, it is natural to resist the thought of death, and cling to our hopes for life. If it has been too much of a mixed bag, and the forecast is for more of the same, death is a bit simpler to contemplate, perhaps easier to accept.

"My vision of death is of sleep. A long, cold sleep. Nothing more. And nothing less," my friend, Nick, told me.

"I think of life as all the things I want to do, have to do before that...sleep. I'm in no hurry for it. But I'm not afraid of it either."

Lovers are haunted by death not only because of the anticipated sorrow and grief, but because of the bleak vision of life without a beloved companion. Doug and Mary Ann, who, in chapter II, related their fantasies and thoughts of getting home to each other to share their day's experiences, have a fantasy that helps them with their fear of parting.

Doug and Mary Ann

"Sometimes in the middle of all the bliss, this ugly thought turns up of what would happen if one of us should die. We've talked about it—how we would face it, how we would live, whether we would remarry. And the prospect would be so depressing, of course, that we would usually wind up in a tearful embrace, or, more often, when the thought or subject came up, we would just quickly dance away from it and try to forget it.

"Until we came up with this perfect solution to the whole problem," continued Mary Ann. "We decided on matching heart attacks, and went into great peals of laughter fantasizing just how and when those heart attacks would occur."

"Our favorite solution was for the great moment to happen just at the point of orgasm," Doug chimed in laughingly. "One great fit of passion, and it's all over for the both of us."

"There are times Doug gets a pained look on his face," Mary Ann continued, "indigestion or something, and I'll say, 'Is this it? Hold on. I'm not ready yet.' And we'll both break up."

A little humor helps. The poet and playwright John Gay, who wrote *The Beggar's Opera*, composed his own epitaph:

Life is a jest; and all things show it.
I thought so once, but now I know it.

Well, life is more than a jest, but if we can remember that jesting is an important part of it, that keeping it light keeps it fresh and tolerable, we can keep away some of the gloom that can descend upon us when we contemplate our mortality.

Death has been lightly described as complete maturity. Before we do become dead ripe, most of us want the chance to savor all we can of life's bounty. If we have a sense of mission, and it is as yet unfulfilled, we will not yield easily to thoughts and fantasies of death. If we want one more turn on the merry-go-round, we will not go in peace.

All wisdom points to making the most of the time we have, and the loves and urges we feel, moment to moment. Our happy involvement with the life we choose will crowd our fears of death out of our fantasy life, and leave much-needed room for the best that's yet to come.

VIII. TOMORROW

I'll think of it all tomorrow....
I can stand it then....
After all, tomorrow is another day.
Margaret Mitchell,
GONE WITH THE WIND

Survivors know all about tomorrow. Tomorrow is our deliverance. Our chance to break free. To get it right. Make it perfect. See our dream come true. Enter Shangri-la. If we are hopeful, faithful, patient, provident, tomorrow is our solace and our salvation.

It is where and when we get *ours*. Most of us have a dream of paradise, that perfect place or time warp we have designed in our heads to which we can retire with honor. When life gets too tiresome and frustrating, we glaze over, hang out the "Do Not Disturb" sign, and drift off.

Our fantasies of paradise may change their time and locale and cast of characters as life goes on, but their allure never varies. No matter how good we have it, things could be better.

Our daydreams of a more glorious tomorrow help us get through today, help us accept our lot with the promise of a new world to come. They are like air rights that hover in perpetuity over our lowly estates. Just knowing they are there is sometimes comfort enough.

Marion teaches history. If richness of imagination,

clearness of vision and great personal warmth are essential to her calling, and they must be, she is an inspiring teacher, one I could have wished for as a guide to the glories of antiquity.

Marion

"My life has been so rich, so full of the deep pleasures I have always derived from reading and imagining and traveling and talking with people, and sharing what I have learned and...*felt* in my teaching and writing. So much of the joy and interest has come from the inside, in savoring the images and feeling the mental and spiritual connections that happen inside when you let your imagination...roam freely over the ideas and events you're trying to assimilate, understand.

"My fantasies, strung end to end, would circle the earth, I'm afraid, but I often think of one that I feel had real significance in my life. It lingered in my imagination for a long, long time, and things grew out of it that led very directly to choices I made about my life. Important choices.

"It goes back to my girlhood and my early school days, west of here in New York State, in the early thirties, and a picture I had come across in a book I was reading. The subject was "The Rape of the Sabines," and I think it was in a book of the history of the Romans.

"The picture itself was an engraving that had been made from a painting, one I think done by an early nineteenth-century French painter, probably David. I had seen the picture before I had read about the Sabines, so that I saw it completely out of context with the details of the legend.

"Now, of course, as a girl of thirteen or fourteen, the word 'rape' was a powerful one. I had only recently learned its significance, and it had been presented to me in somewhat of a...cushioned way, so that it was the object of, well, dread fascination. I knew that it was a criminal act of violence, punishable by death in those days, and that it involved sexual aggression, but all of these terms and ideas really weren't in complete focus for me yet. These days, I'm sure, I would have been considered retarded. But we're talking about the early thirties. And very early Marion.

"The picture itself was a magnificent scene. Here were these monumentally beautiful Sabine women, clad, or almost clad, in those loose, flowing, revealing robes, and posed in these varying states of alarm and...surrender, being swept up into the arms and onto the horses of these huge and heroic Romans. I think there were a few slain bodies lying about, Sabine men, probably. But with all the classical landscape and architecture and the sweep of events so dramatically portrayed, I was deeply stirred.

"Well, needless to say, my desire to read on and find out exactly what this rape was all about was a keen one. And that's precisely what I set out to do. What I discovered, of course, was the legend of the followers of Romulus who, finding themselves in need of wives, swept down upon the Sabines and carried off their women to Rome in the early days of its founding. Later, many of the patricians of Rome claimed to be descended from these Sabine women.

"So much for history. Well, I was fascinated. This was no sordid little back-alley event. This was *history*, this grand carrying off of women to help found an empire. At least that's what sank into my romantic and girlish imagination.

"And it stayed there. I was a...plain little girl, pale and shy and bookish, I'm afraid. And this at a time when all my little friends were blossoming into young beauties and attracting all the boys. And I went through a period of feeling rejected and unworthy of notice. But my reading and my imagination gave me strength and interest, and in my quiet way, I think, I was building my reserves, and...finding my way.

"One of the things that sustained me was this vivid fantasy that some day this band of beautiful Romans would come riding over the crest of the hill and carry me off as one of their brides to this beautiful far away city with its shining white temples and palaces. And there I would be loved and valued and be part of this heroic life of empire and glory.... You can see I still get carried away.

"Well, that fantasy sustained me, let me tell you. And there were little ways I could live it occasionally that nurtured it. Most of the schools in those days had classes in what was called "interpretive dancing" for the girls. They were a carry-over from the days of Isadora Duncan and Denishawn, I think, and we were quite a sight with all of our delicate cavorting. Many of the inspirations for the dances we learned were supposedly Greek and Roman in origin. And we would occasionally give dance recitals, which of course meant costumes. Greek and Roman costumes.

"So there I was, my imagination fairly bursting with these images of myself as this glorious Sabine creature moving airily, seductively about, hoping against hope that in one of my most fetching moments of transport, my Roman would appear. I must tell you, if you will allow me to boast, that I was considered the most gifted dancer in our group, and that I got no small amount of attention for my inspired movements and poses."

"Poses?" I asked.

"Yes, indeed," Marion replied, "poses." Part of all our theatrics were what were called *tableaux vivants*, living pictures. And there we would be, frozen like statues in some group pose that supposedly represented 'Venus Arising' or 'The Vestal Virgins,' or whatever.

"The dancing helped bring me out of my shell somewhat. But somewhere along the way my fascination with history, and particularly classical history, took a deep hold on me. It just seemed like an endless fantasy, let's call it, of heroic beings and great events and pageantry and beauty and terror—all the passions and movements of time were there, always before you, to peruse and study and savor.

"I was an early convert. And I was fortunate enough to have had excellent teachers in history throughout high school and college and later at Columbia. They helped gather me into the fold, so to speak. But quite early, I think, I determined to study and teach. And sure enough, here I am."

I asked Marion if the fantasy of the Romans and the Sabines still worked its magic for her. "In my memory, it's still with me," she replied. "But not, of course, in the same way it was at the beginning of my life. I've thought about it many times, many times since, and I still do. And bits of it still drift into my consciousness from time to time.

"In retrospect, of course, I see the eroticism of it, which I'm sure I felt in those days. And I've often thought, given my feelings of plainness at the time, that my interest in history, particularly of that period, had to be something of a sublimation of my erotic feelings. But it all seemed to happen so inevitably, my interest in history was so genuine, that I never thought of it at the time as anything other than . . . almost a calling.

"I've often made the association that the Romans in a way did carry me off, or perhaps it's more accurate to say I followed them to the big city. Either way, I've enjoyed the thought.

"I didn't exactly find an empire here," Marion laughed. "But I found someone who made me forget my Romans— my wild Irish husband. And, of course, my teaching. Both are my treasures. My children, too."

Marion and her husband both teach at universities in the New York City area. Marion, of course, teaches classical civilization and her husband, English literature. Marion's roads still lead to Rome and Greece, where she spends many of her summers in writing and research for her books.

The beauty, strength, and intellect that characterized Greek and Roman antiquity still glow across the centuries like a vision of paradise, tempting the susceptible. But our great tomorrow can take any shape and form, and it can be a matter of circumstance and condition as much as one of a given time and place.

Barry

Barry is an actor, and a good one, with successes behind him, and hopes ahead for the establishment of a solid career.

"My dream is not of stardom, but of being a constantly working actor, one who is called for, is in demand, is respected and known and used. The worst part of this business is that dreaded in-between time when you're waiting and wondering if anyone will call, whether your last audition was successful, whether there will ever be another play, or film, or commercial.

"It's agony. And it's depressing. But it's part of the game and you have to learn to live with it, relax as best you can, and hope. And it's hard as hell.

"The second-worst part is the trouping around to the casting offices when you do get a call and you go through the endless readings in front of strange, unencouraging-looking people, and worry afterward about how well you did, and whether you thought they liked you or not, and whether they can *use* you this time, and on and on. And you call your answering service every half hour to see if you got the magic call.

"Sometimes when it all gets to me, I will just sit down, or lie down and just psych myself into thinking about what it would be like if I really made it. To know the peace of knowing what you would be doing for the next few years. I fantasize bookings and engagements that would take me from here to Australia and back. And those sweet, calm feelings of knowing who I am, what I'm doing and where I'm going just wash over me.

"I have visions of showing up on sets and having people know who I am, and how good I am, and, in a very unruffled way, delivering the goods with a poise that commands everyone's respect and admiration. It is easy and effortless. One does not sweat. One has a reputation.

"And one does not, under any circumstances, have to

audition. It's a simple matter of knowing Barry is the best. If you're lucky, he's available. Call Barry.

"Well, all of this helps. I've had enough of a taste of it in the past to know that it can happen. Right now I just want it to happen on a continuous basis. When the phone rings, I want them to be asking not if I'm available tomorrow, but whether or not I'll have time to fit a play in between my next two specials. When they do, I'll know I'm in heaven. My heaven."

Barry is preparing for the day when the calls will come in on a steady basis. Till then, his fantasy can help keep his anxieties at bay, and his goal foremost in his mind.

Rick's fantasy is pure self-amusement, shading off into play. Like Marion, he teaches history and has imaginative involvement in the period of his specialty.

Rick

Rick teaches history in a private school in an area rich in colonial history, and lives with his growing young family in a colonial homestead he is in the process of restoring with his own considerable skills.

He is an excellent carpenter and cabinetmaker, and has converted a small building on his property into a woodworking shop. He cuts his own trees, and saws his own lumber from them, leaving the cut planks to season outside the shop. Inside he has an extraordinary collection of woodworking tools, many of them shaping and cutting implements virtually unchanged from their original, centuries-old design.

His specialty is furniture of colonial design. He crafts it of local woods, using many of the same techniques employed by the eighteenth-century cabinetmakers he admires. It is no coincidence that his teaching specialty is American history.

"I've had many enjoyable moments here," he said as he

showed me his studio one evening. "But, as you can imagine, this kind of work takes patience. And it's easy and pleasant to drift off into daydreaming while I'm planing, or shaping or sanding. One of my favorite reveries is to imagine myself back in the eighteenth century working a piece of furniture in much the same way the cabinetmakers of that time plied their craft.

"The music helps get me in the mood," he said, as he pointed to a sound system he had installed. He is a knowledgeable lover of music, and his recordings show strength in the music of the classical period.

"It's so relaxing to me, just drifting off into this pleasant world, removed only in time, really, from this very place. I can spend hours here, and come away feeling refreshed, feeling as though I've been away. And it's wonderful to know it's always here when I need it, or want to enjoy it."

Rick, like most of the people whose fantasies are recorded here, is a person of imagination, one who has survived into maturity with that prize faculty still intact and flourishing. Considering that it seems to have been a long-standing stratagem of many of our parents to draw us out of our imaginative worlds and fling us into reality, it has been heartening to observe just how many of us are holdouts.

Perhaps it's unfair to be testy with our parents in retrospect. We have all seen the results of living too much in fantasy and illusion and having too little commitment and resolution that we act upon.

But is it possible to go overboard into delusions if we have an active fantasy life? Psychologist Jerome Singer thinks not. "Actually there is evidence in the other direction," he says. "People who use fantasy consciously know very well how to test the reality of an experience," he stated in an article in *Vogue* magazine (November 1976).

In another article in *Psychology Today* (July 1976), he stated:

> We often assume that children with active fantasy lives
> have a weaker grasp on hard facts than their pedestrian
> brothers and sisters. But the truth of the matter may be

just the opposite. Research indicates that children whose games are poor in make-believe and fantasy are likely to have trouble recalling and integrating the details of events they hear about.

Singer further suggests that those of us caught up in alcoholism and drug addiction may indeed have "failed to develop an elaborate and satisfying inner life," and may "lack the inner control and quiet sense of purpose that a rich imagination can provide."

Many of the people whose daydreams are related here seemed to have such clear and definite recollections of fantasies from their childhood and early teens. Perhaps since this is a time when we are so impressionable, the vivid ones stay with us as indelibly as the memorable events of reality. Certainly we are less armored at that point in our lives, and perhaps more receptive to and needful of the help that fantasies can bring. Less capable, too, of shrugging off and forgetting the puzzling and bewildering scenarios many of them contain.

In a recent study psychologist Leonard Giambra completed with the Gerontology Research Center of the National Institute on Aging, using over a thousand subjects of all ages, it was observed that men and women tend to daydream about the same things, and that problem solving was the most common theme. Sex was the more common theme with men, except in the thirty-to-thirty-four age group in women, when their sex fantasies rivaled in number those of men.

The study, as reported in *Psychology Today* (October 1977), revealed that daydreaming declines with age, with one sudden spurt upward in the forty-five-to-forty-nine age group, when, perhaps, midlife crises make unusual demands on the attentions of our imaginations. The elderly do not, as has been popularly thought, drift most often into reveries of the past, but daydream equally of the past, present, and future.

The study showed that, at all ages, women daydream more and with greater intensity than men. The reason for this has yet to be determined conclusively. Perhaps it is because, having for so long been denied access to so many activities and areas of interest in life, women have reached out to touch them in the one way that cannot be denied them—through their imaginations.

Of those women with whom I spoke about their fantasies, no one gave a more touching and beautiful narrative than Jean. Her fantasy, like those of several others, was inspired by a film. But she has made it very much her own vision.

Jean

"I saw the film *The Red Shoes* at a very impressionable age, and in a way it opened my life to intensely aesthetic feelings I had never known before. In it, at one point, the central character, a young ballerina, is summoned by the impresario of the company to his villa outside Monte Carlo, high up in the cliffs that overlook the Mediterranean.

"He will tell her, once she is there, that she has been chosen to dance the lead in a newly created ballet, 'The Red Shoes.' He has sent his car for her, an elderly and perfect Rolls-Royce, with an open roof in the back. She is dressed like a princess, with a small diamond coronet and a long cape of blue silk.

"As the car travels slowly on the road that winds along the cliffs, this soft, evocative impressionistic music follows, with a soprano voice softly dominating the sound. The car stops at last at the foot of a long, long staircase of ancient stones that leads high up to a promontory on which the villa sits.

"She lifts her cape slightly and gracefully in front of her and slowly ascends the staircase as the music rises faintly in the background. She reaches the top, approaches a great wrought-iron gate, opens it, and enters a cloistered garden that adjoins the main house of the villa.

"The sky above and the Mediterranean below are incredibly blue. The clouds are very white. The sun is brilliant. And I can see it all quite clearly as I'm telling you this. And feel the cool breeze off the Mediterranean."

"I have climbed those stairs a thousand times in my imagination, and each time seems more real than the last. What I feel is perfect beauty filling every sense. And feelings of expectation and promise and of being in touch with something eternal.

"I have long since dropped the plot and the circumstance of the story. What I have done is internalize all those early sensations of beauty and emotion I felt so intensely when I first saw the film.

"There are times that I imagine I am climbing those stairs to what I think of as paradise, and that I will open that gate and enter into a vast open temple, and I will see and feel and touch God.

"I feel such a sweet peace in this fantasy. It has brought me many moments of glorious feeling. I have little idea of its meaning. I never want to know. I know everything I want to know about it already."

Our world has been altered forever by mathematics and science and the rich and imaginative creativity through which they will continue to advance us into the universe. At times we seem to be hurtled along at such force that we lose the sense of our humanity and our unique identity. Nowhere can they be more quickly revived than in that realm where we alone can claim sovereignty—our imaginations.

There we live and dream and plan and solve and fortify ourselves against the unknown. It is there we plan the commitments that will carry our life forward and enable us to do what we must do. What must we do? Bernard Iddings Bell, in his book, *Crisis in Education* (Whittlesey House, 1949), urged this:

Man exists to do creatively, in the most craftsmanlike manner possible, all things that must be done: great things like government, or mothering, or the healing of minds and bodies; small things like making beds, or hoeing corn, or driving a truck.... There are a vast number of tasks to be performed in this world, most of them not romantic. They may be done in one of two ways: just to get them over with as quickly and as painlessly as possible, in which case they become a monotonous burden hard to bear; or each as beautifully and thoroughly as possible, in which case life is good to the taste.

To *do* creatively, we must first imagine ourselves as creative and worthwhile doers. Surely that is a simple task. As simple as putting our fantasies to work for us.

INDEX